The Family Daughter

"In this utterly transparent book, Sarah Bryant speaks from her heart about the daily walk of the daughter at home. Sharing her own struggles and triumphs, Sarah demonstrates that it is grace that animates our calling as godly women and that God is faithful to equip us as we joyfully submit to His sanctifying power... I was not only refreshed by Sarah's honest words; I was convicted anew of areas I need to work on as a wife and mother! If you are a daughter at home, this book will encourage you to pursue the Lord's work with new vision. Including testimonies from many other young women, *The Family Daughter* doesn't paint an unrealistic picture of perfection but deals with the reality of our sin nature in the light of Christ's promises to His people. I'd also highly recommend this book to mothers as a glimpse into the heart of a daughter. I found Sarah's insights helpful as I ponder how to wisely bring up my own daughters. Thank you, Sarah, for this beautiful labor of love for your sisters in Christ!"

—Mrs. Jennie Chancey
Homemaker, Founder of Ladies Against Feminism,
Co-Author of *Passionate Housewives Desperate For God*

"This is just the encouragement I have been praying for, and have so desperately needed these past few months of spiritual drought! I can see so clearly the humility and willingness to be led by the Holy Spirit in your writing, and that is what makes it valuable: the fact that Jesus Christ shines through every word, causing people to look beyond you and the other girls who contributed. He is what will make this work effective. Well done, and thank you so much!"

—Grace Pennington
Daughter at Home, Producer of *Journey of Honor* Documentary

"*The Family Daughter* is an excellent book for Christian young ladies. Through practical Scriptural applications and personal testimonies from single young women, readers will realize that marriage is not a goal to be attained before they can find and do God's will—their lives can be full of joy, purpose, potential and fulfillment right now!"

—Mrs. Kari Lewis
Homemaker, Co-Founder of *Home School Enrichment Magazine*

"*The Family Daughter* has been such an encouragement to me already! I was reminded several times of the importance of humbly serving, living wholeheartedly for Jesus instead of the world. I was refreshed by the positive viewpoint you maintained and the many godly stories and testimonies you shared. *The Family Daughter* won't just challenge daughters' relationships with family—but it will also challenge their relationship with their Savior, which is truly the foundation of everything else in life. How wonderful to have both in one book!"

—Tiffany Schlichter
Daughter at Home,
Author of *Noble Girlhood* and *All Glorious Within*

The Family Daughter

BECOMING PILLARS *of* STRENGTH
IN OUR FATHER'S HOUSE

by SARAH L. BRYANT

THE FAMILY DAUGHTER
— *Becoming Pillars of Strength in Our Father's House*

COPYRIGHT ©2010 *KBR Ministries*. All rights reserved.

This book is protected by copyright; however, we welcome the sharing of an occasional page for edification of friends—provided source and ordering information are given.

KBR MINISTRIES is a ministry designed to encourage young ladies to grow in accordance with Titus Two and Proverbs 31:10-31, in obedience to God and their parents. See page 204 to read about our other resources, or contact us at:

21350 Springdale Road, Easton, Kansas 66020
editor@kingsbloomingrose.com
www.kingsbloomingrose.com

PRINTED in the United States of America

FIRST PRINTING · 2010

ISBN · 978-1-4507-1792-2

SCRIPTURE QUOTATIONS · King James Version of *The Holy Bible*

PROOFREADERS · Dana Bryant, Thomas Bryant, Jennie Chancey, Jennie Chandler, Kari Lewis, Grace Pennington, Tiffany Schlichter, Dr. Randall Talbot

BOOK DESIGN · Sarah L. Bryant

PHOTOGRAPHY · ©*SarahLee Photography* unless otherwise noted; see page 202

FRONT COVER · Sarah & Rachael Bryant

Dedicated to

MY PARENTS
who have invested so much in my life.
Your sacrifices have been great,
& I am ever grateful; future generations
will also rise up and call you blessed.

MY SISTER RACHAEL
I pray you will be the strong pillar
in your home that God desires of you!
Let Jesus conform you into His image—
& press heavenward always.

table of CONTENTS

PREFACE	As Cornerstones	PAGE 15
CHAPTER 1	An Abundant Season	PAGE 21
CHAPTER 2	In My Father's House	PAGE 29
CHAPTER 3	Our Parents' Joy	PAGE 51
CHAPTER 4	The Family Sister	PAGE 69
CHAPTER 5	Pillars of Strength	PAGE 93
CHAPTER 6	A Humble Maidservant	PAGE 117
CHAPTER 7	The Spotless Maiden	PAGE 135
CHAPTER 8	The Appointed Time	PAGE 157
CHAPTER 9	Reflecting The Light	PAGE 171
CHAPTER 10	Bouquet of Beauty	PAGE 191

Background | 12
Acknowledgments | 13

Endnotes | 200
Story of This Book | 202
About the Author | 203
KBR Ministries | 204
Order Form | 205

Some BACKGROUND

THE PERSPECTIVE from which this book was written is based on the following Scriptural beliefs:

- Women were created to be a help-meet to their husband if married (Titus 2:5), or serve their father if unmarried (Genesis 24)
- An unmarried daughter should remain under the authority of her father until he passes that authority to another godly man whom God has prepared for her (Genesis 2:24 and I Corinthians 7:36-38)
- An unmarried daughter should follow Biblical models of daughterhood by honoring parents (Exodus 20:12), encouraging her family (Psalm 144:12), and remaining spotless from the world in thoughts, conduct, and reputation (James 1:27)
- A wife should love her husband, raise children for the glory of God, and adorn herself with a meek and quiet spirit (I Peter 3:4, Titus 2:5)

Please use the Holy Scriptures as your guide throughout this book—through faith comes understanding of the things of God (I Peter 1:5, Hebrews 11:1,3).

Acknowledgements
THANK YOU

I AM FOREMOST indebted to the Lord Jesus Christ, Who gives meaning to my life, Who guides my feet, and Who holds my future. Thank you, Jesus, for your ultimate sacrifice, so that it is possible that I may be conformed into Your image.

Thank you to my dear parents, who have guided and taught me Truth. Thank you for caring enough to make a difference—choosing to raise us for God's glory. I appreciate all the time you have taken to edit this book.

I am thankful for each of my siblings, Brandon, Nathan, Jonathan, Rachael and Samuel. You are such an incredible blessing in my life and I learn so much from you!

Many thanks to the young ladies who have mentored, encouraged, and blessed me by their godly lives. Your Christ-like examples have laid a visual example of inspiration. I am passing on the gems of wisdom you have shared with me throughout this book.

I also would like to extend my gratitude to each of the young ladies who shared their testimonies and thoughts throughout each chapter. A huge thanks to the many kind friends who took time to proofread the manuscript and offer invaluable feedback.

Thank *you* for reading this book. I would love to hear your testimony. *Soli Deo Gloria!*

A Good DAUGHTER

There are other ministries of love more conspicuous than hers,
But none in which a gentler, lovelier spirit dwells,
And none 'twich the heart more joyfully responds.
As son's occupations carry him more abroad,
While a good daughter is the *steady light* of her father's house.
Her idea is indissolubly connected with that of his happy fireside.
She is his morning sunlight and his evening star
The grace and vivacity and the tenderness of her sex
Have their place in the mighty sway which she holds over his spirit.
The lessons of recorded wisdom which he reads with her eyes
Come to his mind with a new charm
As they blend with the *beloved* melody of her voice.

He scarcely knows weariness which her song does not make him forget,
Or gloom which is proof of the young brightness of her smiles
She is the pride and ornament of his hospitality
And the *gentle* nurse of his sickness,
The constant agent in those nameless numberless acts of kindness
Which one chiefly cares to have rendered
Because they are unpretending, but all-expressive of her love.
And then what a cheerful share is she
And what an able lightener of a mother's cares.
What an ever-present **delight** and triumph to a mother's affection.

Oh, how little do those *daughters* know
Of the power which God has committed to them!
And the happiness that a *parent's* eye that rests on them
    Bring rapture to a parent's heart.

[AUTHOR UNKNOWN]

PREFACE

As CORNERSTONES

Dear Sisters,

ON OUR PROPERTY, the stone foundation and pillars of a structure linger. These had been the strength of the building and endured many years of harsh weather, though the structure itself had fallen away. The scenes this deserted site had seen remained untold, but one thing stood out clearly—it had prevailed against the foes of nature!

Last summer, as I slowly climbed over this foundation and gazed at the tall cornerpillars, this desolate scene suddenly seemed to come alive as a phrase came to mind—"polished cornerstones." The Lord reminded me of that beautiful verse found in Psalm 144:12: *"That our daughters may be as corner stones, polished after the similitude of a palace."* I was struck with the visual picture of what I, as a daughter, should be in my home—a strong and faithful support to the structure in which the Lord has placed me. What a vivid picture this Scripture paints of the beautifying and vital role a daughter has in her home.

Our Purpose

In Genesis 2:18, we find that God created women specifically for the purpose of helping man: "*The Lord God said, It is not good that the man should be alone; I will make him a help meet for him.*" The woman's role is to be a help-meet to her husband, keeper at home, and mother. Titus 2:4-5 says, "*That they may teach the young women to be sober, to love their husbands, to love their children, to be discreet, chaste, keepers at home, good, obedient to their own husbands.*"

Biblical examples demonstrate that daughters remained under their father's authority until their marriage.[1] Daughters, while under their father's protection, served their family with fidelity. For example, in Genesis 24, Rebekah was diligently serving in her father's house when God brought her a husband. Her heart of service was a sign to Abraham's servant that she was the woman to be Isaac's wife. During this season, she was also preparing herself for the calling she would undertake as a wife to Isaac and mother to many.

Rachel, in Genesis 29, was under her father's protection tending to his flock when she met her future husband, Jacob. What a beautiful picture her example is, as she contentedly served her father through the humble task of caring for his sheep.

Though the World[2] expects the twenty-first century girl to move out of her father's house and support herself with a career, as Christians we must look to the principles found in God's Word. Only when we are following God's plan will we truly find peace, knowing we are in His will. His plan for us is a joyous, stimulating, and success-filled mission.

Daughters of Grace

Back to the verse, Psalm 144:12: "*That our daughters may be as corner stones, polished after the similitude of a palace.*" What is a cornerstone?

According to Noah Webster, it is "the stone which lies at the corner of two walls, and unites them."[3] Clearly, parents are the main structure in a family, but an honoring daughter can lift much of their burden by uniting efforts and lending support. We, as daughters, cannot begin to understand how much responsibility our parents carry, especially our father who has been called to spiritually lead and physically provide for his family. When our parents know that we want to help them and support their mission, they will be blessed and strengthened.

Imagine a pillar in a beautiful palace: uplifting and beautifying. A pillar is "a supporter; that which sustains or upholds; that on which some superstructure rests."[4] If we are to be our family's strength and pillar, we must be present under the protection of the structure—our family—we are supporting. Our presence as a daughter has a great influence in the family, and we can choose to use this power to build up or tear down our family.[5] By upholding and honoring our parents, we grace their home as a pillar of strength, and by following God's plan for us, we can help make our family's abode a lovely palace of refuge.

A Journey Together

Although these things may sound good and even simple to you, maybe you feel you can never be that "ideal" daughter. The idea of being a pillar in your home may seem so far-fetched, that you do not even hope to obtain the goal. Does it seem the vision for godly daughterhood is only for "perfect daughters"? Dear sister, I too, have felt that despair. Before the Lord turned my heart to my authority and gave me a vision for daughterhood, I thought the idea of joyfully honoring my father could never be a reality in *my* life! I resigned myself to the thought that only "good girls" could be that way. It was not until I was almost fifteen that the Lord worked a miraculous change in my heart. Through a series of events and months, the Lord turned my heart toward home and to my family. I praise the Lord that He has begun this work in my heart; I am ever grateful that my Lord promises to complete the purification which He has begun in my life—and this is a continuous *daily* process. *"Not as though I had already attained, either were already perfect: but I follow after, if that I may apprehend that for which also I am apprehended of Christ Jesus"* (Philippians 3:12).

I am confident God can do the same transformation in your life, for this is promised in Philippians 1:6: *"Being confident of this very thing, that he which hath begun a good work in you will perform it until the day of Jesus Christ."* It is never too late, dear sister, to turn your heart to your father. It is not too late to start loving your family, to embrace the potential you have in your home as a daughter. This simply requires the surrender and humility to ask God to transform you. God's work in your life may seem to be a slow process, and in truth, this will be a continual life-work as He transforms you more into His likeness. As we continually seek God's Word and welcome His hand in our life, He will make us *"perfect in every good work to do His will"* (Hebrews 13:21). In this way, our loving Father will make each of us more polished for His palaces.

I do not write as if I have attained anything; I only want to encourage you to join me on this journey. I desire to share what the Lord has taught me so you can learn from my mistakes. My heart goes out to you who are leaving behind your girlhood, and entering the blessed season of womanhood—what a critical season in life this is for you. The choices you make today will impact your life, your family, and your future progeny. I encourage you to embrace your noble role as a daughter and to delight in His will! Do not settle for anything less, no matter what the odds may seem. Let us press upward together, becoming a pillar of strength in our father's house.

YOUR SISTER,

Sarah Lee

April 2010

"We will have all of eternity to celebrate the *victories won*, & only a few short hours before sunset TO WIN THEM."

[AMY CARMICHAEL]

"Not that I speak in respect of want — for I have *learned*, in *whatsoever state I am*, therewith to be CONTENT."

[PHILIPPIANS 4:11]

CHAPTER ONE

AN ABUNDANT *Season*

$\mathcal{E}$VERY GIRL DREAMS of caring for her own baby someday. At a young age, she loves cuddling her doll and dreaming of names for her little "baby." I remember caring for a room full of dolls when I was younger; in fact, I still have these dolls I used to play with. Yet as I have grown older, they have remained stuffed in my closet for longer lengths of time as my dreams have taken greater depth. The Lord has given me a vision to be a wife, mother, and godly homemaker, as revered in the Bible. More of my time is now spent developing skills that will be useful as a future homemaker. Upon the day of marriage, I will not suddenly be equipped for the responsibility a homemaker carries; I must gird myself in preparation today.

Let us look at the parable Jesus gives in Matthew chapter 25, about the ten virgins who awaited their bridegroom. Five virgins foolishly did not prepare for their coming groom. The other five kept their lamps trimmed and had extra oil—and it was these who were ready when their bridegroom appeared in the night. The five foolish maids were left to scamper around to find oil for their dimming lamps, so that they missed their long-awaited bridegroom. In fact, when they finally arrived late at the wedding, they were utterly cast away—their bridegroom did not even recognize them: *"I say unto you, I know you not"* (Matthew 25:12).

In a similar way, we are maidens awaiting both our heavenly and earthly groom, and we can find truth and admonition from this parable. We need to prepare for the tasks that may lay ahead of us, and not fritter away this season, so that we will be ready for whatever the Lord calls us to do. Though we may greatly long for the time when we can marry, we need to wisely use this opportunity to prepare for the next. We must remain content where the Lord currently has us, preparing instead of pining. We can find rest and peace in being content, trusting that God has a perfect plan for our futures, as Jeremiah 29:11 promises, *"I know the thoughts that I think toward you, saith the LORD, thoughts of peace."*

"True contentment will only come as I learn to wait on the Lord and seek His face. The Lord is the only One who can satisfy the longing in our souls, as Psalm 107:9 says. It is only the Lord who can give me the ability to truthfully say *'I delight to do thy will, O my God'* (Psalm 40:8)."

—Anna Kirk (19), Daughter at Home

At times, it has been a struggle in my own life to keep my heart content. I went through a particular time when I incessantly worried, "What if I never get married?" I became so overwhelmed that I could not cope with today's calling to *prepare myself* to be keeper at home. The Lord opened my eyes to the truth: I was not trusting His timing for my life, and if I am not content in this season of singlehood, I will definitely not be content after marriage. One friend put it this way,

> "Christ is the only one who can fulfill my longings and desires. No husband can. It is hard to explain the glorious sense of nearness I have with my heavenly Bridegroom, Christ. We should indeed delight to be with Him in the same way a maiden delights in her bridegroom."

CHAPTER ONE — *An Abundant Season*

When Christ's will is our highest ambition, we will find fulfillment. When Christ is first in our life, our best friend, closest confidant, and our deepest desire, we will find contentment in whatever He has for our life. Instead of impatiently waiting for a husband, we will find great value in investing in this precious relationship with our Savior.

When I become fearful or discontent, I must pray, "Lord, I give up my dreams of my future. I know you will use these years to prepare and mold me into a vessel for Your use." Surrendering my dreams has given me a peace *"that passeth all understanding"* (Philippians 4:7). It has been freeing for me to simply trust the Lord for my future, and since I have committed this specific area to Him, I have also been able to more wholeheartedly follow my dad where he leads. As long as I am serving and following the Lord by doing this, He will bless my efforts!

I have found one of the best remedies for maintaining an attitude of contentment is to simply focus on the tasks God has given me to do, thus, avoiding thoughts that cause me to struggle with this desire for something I do not yet have. I have to choose to let my desire for marriage rest. *"I charge you, O ye daughters of Jerusalem...that ye stir not up, nor awake my love, till he please"* (Song of Solomon 2:7). I want to encourage you, dear sister, to look to the Lord for the things He has for you today. We can and should look forward to the day when we may undertake the blessed role of homemaker, but we must remain content where He has us today and the tasks He has for us during this season.

We should not to fuel the desire for marriage by feeding our minds with media that stimulates this craving. This can be a difficult choice; it means we guard every single thought! A married lady recently shared with me that she had to learn, while single, to not stir up her desire for marriage. She used the illustration of a jar of water containing sparkles—when she shakes the jar they are stirred and "come alive," but when she lets it rest in peace, they settle. Until the right time, when Lord brings along a mate, we must be careful not to stir up these emotions.

God knows every detail of our future; His plan is much superior to ours. No matter what He may have for our life, we must trust that our Lord knows best, even if it means sacrificing the dearest desires of our heart. *"Commit thy works unto the LORD, and thy thoughts shall be established"* (Proverbs 16:3). When we follow Him, we will find that the hardest trials and our deepest sacrifices actually add the most vibrant colors to the picture of life. If we only trust Him, our Father will fulfill our dreams much more extraordinarily than we can imagine—because He has an infinitely greater perspective.

The time we have before marriage[1] is a wonderful opportunity we have been given to serve the Lord, bless our family, and prepare ourselves to lead a mission-driven life for His glory. We must embrace it! Ephesians 5:15 warns all who will hear, *"See then that ye walk circumspectly, not as fools, but as wise."* This season in life contains incredible potential, since we as girls have the energy to invest in projects that as a wife and mother we may not have the opportunity nor time. I Corinthians 7:34 points this out, *"The unmarried woman careth for the things of the Lord, that she may be holy both in body and in spirit: but she that is married careth for the things of the world, how she may please her husband."*

Will we prepare like the five wise virgins? When our Bridegroom calls, will He find a prepared maid? May we use this opportunity wisely!

on my shelf... RELATED RESOURCES

— *Keepers at Home: A Handbook for Young Ladies* by Mrs. Susan Zakula (Keepers of the Faith, P.O. Box 100, Ironwood, MI 49938; *www.keepersofthefaith.com*)

— *So Much More* by Anna Sofia & Elizabeth Botkin (The Vision Forum Inc., 4719 Blanco Road, San Antonio, TX 76212; *www.visionforum.com*)

a family daughter...
ABIGAIL M. PAUL

*A*S A SINGLE GIRL still living at home with the big "3-0" just a few months away, the lesson of joyful contentment is part of my daily "homework" from God. Much of the time it is easy; other days, not so easy. I certainly have much yet to learn, but would like to prayerfully share a foundational truth that has been helpful to me throughout this season.

Like most of you, I am blessed to have been raised in a conservative Christian, homeschooling family. My mom never worked outside the home, and devoted all of her time to keeping the household running smoothly, teaching school to the six of us, and doing the million and one things that fill a stay-at-home mom's life to overflowing. I grew up hearing and reading all the teachings about wife and motherhood being a woman's highest calling, and in time I came to embrace that as my own dream for the future. This is all well and good, and I want to be sure to make it clear that I believe it is a very Scripturally-sound, God-honoring dream for girls to have. But what happens when the years keep ticking by and the dream is still unfulfilled? Does this mean we singles are left with a second-rate role in God's service, forced to never accomplish our purpose for living?

Before we can answer this question, we have to realize the difference between a *dream* and a *life goal*. A life goal is our over-arching, all-encompassing reason for living: that for which we would be willing to die, if necessary. It is the source of our motivation for perseverance through discouragement and the push that gets us back on our feet every time we stumble. The apostle Paul summed up his life goal by saying, "For me, to live is Christ, and to die is gain" (Philippians 1:21).

By contrast, dreams are specific ideas of how we would like to translate this goal into practical reality. They are the *how* of the *why*, so to speak. The desire to be a wife and mother fits into this category. Dreams sometimes need to be changed and refined as the years go by, but our life goal should always remain the same: to honor and glorify God.

It is by reminding myself of my life goal that I have been able to gain victories in the battle for contentment. As much as I desire to be a wife and mother, and as sincerely as I believe that it is a God-given, God-honoring dream, it is *not* my life goal. Living my life to honor and glorify God, serving Him however He leads, is my goal. And because I have chosen to call Jesus my Lord, He has prerogative to choose where He would like me to serve Him. If in His love and wisdom He sees that I will best be able to serve Him as a single today, then I do well to accept that assignment without question. I must trust that whatever He chooses is best. If singleness is His gift for me again tomorrow, it will be good. If He sees best to use me in another role tomorrow, such as opening the door for marriage, that will also be good. His way is always better than my way, and His timing is always perfect, even when I do not understand.

As I have gradually come to more deeply realize the truth of this perspective, I have found a much greater ability to embrace all that God has given me today. Every day I am surrounded by opportunities to fulfill my life goal, both in "large" and "small" ways. For me personally, this has thus far meant that I am continuing to live at home with my family, embracing the work and ministry opportunities God has placed before me. By keeping my life goal in view and intentionally pursuing it, I no longer feel that my life is "on hold" while I continue to wait for the gifts of marriage and motherhood. I am able to maintain those dreams without cynicism or bitterness because they are not my focus, and I can entrust them to God for future fulfillment as He deems best.

I am as prone to impatience and distractions as anyone, and this is an area where I need to consistently "speak the truth" to myself. Sometimes it seems I need to remind myself to keep the right focus pretty much on a moment-by-moment basis. But this habit of guarding thoughts and maintaining an eternal perspective will reap benefits all throughout life, whether we marry at a young age or end up serving God as a single our entire life. And there is such a deep *joy* in knowing that I am in the center of God's will for me today! This is the pathway of peace and contentment, and it is very blessed.

May God richly bless you, my sisters, as you continue to wholeheartedly serve God right where He has placed you. Life with Jesus in control is an amazing adventure, and He does have good plans for you. Keep shining!

ABIGAIL PAUL *(29) enjoys life with her parents and younger siblings on their central Iowa farm. Freelance graphic design keeps her busy, along with music, writing, and fellowshipping with her church family.*

"To be discreet, chaste,
keepers at home,
good, **obedient** *to their own husbands, that the*
word of God be not blasphemed."

[TITUS 2:5]

"Even though none of us girls will carry on the earthly name of our father, we will carry on his legacy. I am praying that *my father's vision* will be carried faithfully through my posterity until the coming of Christ, be that ten thousand years from now."[1]

[HANNAH ZES]

CHAPTER TWO

In My FATHER'S HOUSE

AS A DAUGHTER abides in her father's house during her maiden years, she must prepare for the role she may someday face as a wife and keeper at home. She needs to be fully equipped to be a submissive wife, as God sets each woman under the headship of a man. I Corinthians 11:3 explains, "*The head of every man is Christ; and the head of the woman is the man; and the head of Christ is God.*" If we are not submissive to the jurisdictions which God has ordained over us, serious consequences will result, and a godly example will not be set for our future children.

When we accept Christ's sacrifice for our sins, we accept His authority in our life. God has also appointed authorities in the nation, church, and family. Biblically, a family is governed under the leadership of the husband, who is then accountable to the Lord. The roles of the wife and daughter beautifully complete and complement the family unit:

God——Father——Mother——Son/*Daughter*

God——Husband——*Wife*——Children

Parents are in the "chain of command," so to speak. A daughter is under the authority of her head, her father, and upon marriage, this authority is transferred to her husband. An unmarried daughter should learn to honor her father's leadership.[2] This is not only obeying the fifth commandment in Exodus 20:12, "*Honor thy father and thy mother,*" but it is also preparing her for joyful submission to a future husband. What a blessing is the guidance of a Christian father! I am so grateful for my Dad's willingness to protect me and teach me truth—I don't know what I would do without his wisdom. Too often, I take this tremendous gift for granted. We should be so thankful for the blessing of a godly father.

Regardless of whether the Lord calls us to single or married lives, we must gird ourselves with preparation during these formative years in our father's house. While there would be nothing lost if we prepare and the Lord does *not* have marriage for our life, there is a great deal to lose if we do marry and are not ready. Our duty is therefore to learn to joyfully serve and submit to our father, in preparation for the role of a wife. In the Scriptures, we find commands for wives concerning the marriage relationship. We, as daughters, also can find guidance through these words, by applying these principles to our current headship. Wives are commanded to revere their husband in Ephesians 5:33, to submit to him in Colossians 3:18, and to obey him as Sarah did Abraham, in I Peter 3:6. These are a few more key verses pertaining to a woman's role:

> "Wives, submit yourselves unto your own husbands, as it is fit in the Lord. Children, obey your parents in all things: for this is well pleasing unto the Lord." (Colossians 3:18, 20)

> "The aged women likewise, that they be in behavior as becometh holiness, not false accusers, not given to much wine, teachers of good things; That they may teach the young women to be sober, to love their husbands, to love their children, To be discreet, chaste, keepers at home, good, obedient to their own husbands, that the word of God be not blasphemed." (Titus 2:3-5)[3]

Proverbs 31:12 says that the virtuous woman does her husband good *all the days of her life*—and that implies the reputation she brings into her marriage. Obviously, we do not have to wait until we are married to apply these admonitions, and we can prepare ourselves for this role we may undertake in the future. What are some ways that we as daughters can honor our authority? The verses of Proverbs 31 vividly describe a virtuous woman's role; these principles can be gleaned and applied during our maiden years.

- *"The heart of her husband doth safely trust in her."* We likely do not realize how much it means to our parents if they can completely trust the heart of their daughter. We should be trustworthy with projects assigned to us and honest in all situations. Our parents should be assured that when we are out of their sight, we honor their wishes. This character trait, when developed in our life, will be carried into marriage, so that our husband also will be able to completely trust us. What a priceless blessing this will be to him!

- *"She seeketh wool, and flax, and worketh willingly with her hands."* Under our mother's teaching, we have the perfect opportunity to learn these useful skills in managing a home. We can diligently assist her in caring for our family; there are many ways we can be an asset in helping run the home smoothly. We should seek to do everything we put our hands to well—to the best of our ability. It can be so easy to half-way clean up the kitchen, do our chores, or clear off our desk. But God's standard is *perfect*. He never cuts corners. He wants us to do the best that we can do for His glory. I am striving to remind myself more often, *Did I do this task in a way that would please the Lord Himself?* Doing everything *"as to the Lord"* (Colossians 3:23) will be a blessing to our family and set a good example!

- *"She stretcheth out her hand to the poor; yea, she reacheth forth her hands to the needy."* A kind and compassionate heart is of great value, both to the Lord and those around us. Our parents probably do not have much time to do extra things for the needy; since we have less responsibilities than they, we can help them provide assistance as the Lord leads. The virtuous woman brings honor to her authority; by ministering to others in the name of our father, we bring him a good reputation. Through our compassion for those in need, our family's sphere of influence can be greatly extended.

— *"She openeth her mouth with wisdom; and in her tongue is the law of kindness."* Our words have incredible consequences, so rather than tearing down our family members by harsh words and tones, we should use kind words to bless them and promote unity. Learning to control our words will also be a great blessing in a future marriage, as we meekly submit to our husband.

— *"Favour is deceitful, and beauty is vain: but a woman that feareth the* L ORD*, she shall be praised."* Our love for the Lord will be a great blessing especially to our parents—the Bible declares there is no greater joy than seeing one's children walking in the ways of the Lord (3 John 1:4). Our actions will be determined by our reverential fear, or lack thereof, of the Lord. When we truly revere the Lord, we also will be content with His plan for our life.

The most important aspect of honoring our father is that we have committed our heart to his keeping, and are resting in his protection.[4] This can be difficult to do, so if we are not joyful in the authority of our father, we must seek the Lord for a change of heart: *"Search me, O God, and know my heart: try me, and know my thoughts"* (Psalm 139:23). Are we resting in the decisions our dad makes? Are we joyfully supporting his wishes in all areas? Sister, it is very important we learn this lesson now, because we will face it throughout life. We will continually have to learn to more joyfully submit to the authority God has ordained over us, whether it be our father now, or our husband in future marriage. Do not be discouraged if this is a struggle for you. I encourage you to start by honoring your father today—while you are young. I know at times it can be difficult to accept the decisions our fathers make; many girls have told me, "I don't understand why he made that choice!" We do not have to know the reasons behind the decisions our parents make. Our role is to *trust* them with these areas. These responsibilities weigh more heavily on their shoulders than we understand, and if we do not support them, we will add to their burden.

In my own life, being at peace in my dad's leadership is not always easy. One area which I have struggled with is regarding our family moving. As we have searched for a home with more property, it has been difficult for me to rest in the decisions Dad makes. Many times, his choices have not been what I would have preferred. Yet, the Lord showed me that *he* is responsible to follow God's will—what an important task! I definitely do not

> *"You are the key* of the success of your father. You can change a man's life through your devotion and through your comfort; through your hugs, your foot rubs, gentle words, adoring looks, and a true heart that is united...You can change the world by being a comfort to your father, by loving your father!"[5]
>
> —Doug Phillips

want to hinder my dad's obedience to God by having an unsupportive attitude—and so as I have chosen to submit to my dad's leadership and accept his decisions without complaint, I have found such peace. It is relieving to know that as long as I am doing my duty to support Dad, God can work out my fears about the situation. He is in control; I must only obey and trust! I desire to start learning this lesson of trust and submission now, because it will not go away once I am married. This is a heart-issue which will show itself repeatedly. My dad often reminds me that if a daughter does not rest in her father's leadership, she certainly will *not* trust her husband's.

The attitude we show toward our father is incredibly important. Do we show our father love, care, concern, and respect? The Lord has been showing me that I can work all day long and do countless tasks for my dad—but if I am not doing it cheerfully, from my heart, what good have I done? It is vain in the eyes of the Lord. *"Though I speak with the tongues of men and of angels, and have not charity, I am become as sounding brass...And though I bestow all my goods to feed the poor...and have not charity, it profiteth me nothing"* (I Corinthians 13:1). The prophet Micah proclaimed, *"Will the LORD be pleased with thousands of rams, or with ten thousands of rivers of oil?... What doth the LORD require of thee, but to do justly, and to love mercy, and to walk humbly with thy God"* (Micah 6:7-8). King David noted in Psalm 40:6, *"Sacrifice and offering thou didst not desire."* These great men of God knew He desired their heart, their love, rather than empty acts of sacrifice. We must serve our authority from our heart of love. I know I fall short of this goal so often and need to focus more on showing my father a spirit of true thankfulness and love—*does Dad know I stand behind his hard work? Does he know I appreciate his diligence to rise early each morning to provide for his family?*

As I consider the responsibilities my father carries, I am spurred even more to support him wholeheartedly. I do not have to think about holding a paying job as he does, meeting the family's needs, being directly accountable to God, or instructing children in the Lord. All these things, plus much more, my father daily carries on his mind. I do not think we daughters realize how much it weakens the ability of our father if we do not joyfully honor his decisions. If he does not

> *"More than just keep* the home tidy and clean, you are to see to it that the very aroma of sweetness, cheerfulness, and servanthood infuses into every single cranny of the house. Your face is to lighten up and beautify all things, and your mission is to make your father's home the brightest, most cheerful abode on earth."[6]
>
> —Hannah Zes, Daughter at Home

CHAPTER TWO — *In My Father's House*

have the support of his family, he will become discouraged as he tries to merely fix problems within his home. But if a father has the combined support and talents of every family member, what a potent instrument the family can be for the Lord! How we choose to use our influence as daughters has *great* consequences—it can impact the very Kingdom of God. Never think your attitude is of little importance or the way you treat your father does not matter.

Things like showing an interest in our father's job or interests, and just being willing to listen, can bless him more than we might estimate. I encourage you to ask about your dad's projects, even if it is an area in which you have no knowledge or personal interest. Although I do not understand much about my dad's day job, I try to ask him what he is working on, and I really enjoy hearing about the things he has overcome there. It makes me all the more thankful for all that he does. Show you care about what your dad has to say, that you want to hear how you can help lighten his load. Another thing we can do to bless our father is to be loyal to him, no matter the circumstances. One of my friends is especially loyal to her father, even though she is sometimes laughed at by friends for helping him with his business. Let your dad know you stand for him and support his projects. So few in this world are loyal to their family members, so when we do this, we will not only strengthen our father, but we will also be a great witness to others.

Along with resting in our father's authority and demonstrating a cheerful attitude, we can bless our dad by assisting him in many ways. Because my dad works at a full-time job, I used to think I did not have many ways I could really help him physically. When I began to search for opportunities, I found many areas for which I can take responsibility. I also realized most of the ways I can assist my dad are indirect, such as helping around the home while he is away at work. It seems so much more heroic and glorious to serve our father through some "big" responsibility or by being a vital part in his job or ministry. It has been tempting at times for me to compare myself to other girls who are doing what seems to be "big and important" or noticeable tasks for their dads and think, *I don't have any important way to help my dad! I'm just a young girl—what can I do? My help doesn't amount to much compared to the all 'so and so' does for her father in his projects.* This was a struggle for me in past years; I didn't see anything "glorious" I could do for *my* dad like other girls were doing.

The Lord showed me that in His sight, the "small" humble services done in secret are just as important as those big, noticeable projects. If I truly honor and serve Dad from my heart, it does not matter how important what I am doing for him might seem. Our motive must be obedience to God, not recognition for ourselves. You *can* serve your dad in an important way. Anything you do for him is important to God! Do not compare your situation to another girls'; look to the needs of your own family. Sister, if you have a father and live in his home, you have all the opportunities to honor him that any other daughter has for her father. We must not seek glory for ourselves or the fame of the world, for in God's eyes that amounts to nothing. If we seek to honor our father in every thing we do, even if no one else notices, the Lord is pleased.

Every daughter can find areas to serve and honor her dad, though each situation differs. Being cheerful to do the small things for your father may make him willing to give you bigger tasks. Watch for opportunities to do things for him, and this will show your honor and love. My friend Rebekah, age sixteen, has learned even though she may not be able to serve her father in a family home business, she can still honor him in everyday areas:

— Stick a goody such as candy or gum in his lunch bag
— Slip a note in his suitcase or Bible
— Surprise him by doing extra jobs
— Greet him pleasantly when he arrives home from work
— Listen to him share his heart and preach sermons

Another daughter shared with me ways she honors her daddy,
— Greet him every morning
— Make his breakfast and pack his lunch on weekdays
— Keep the house neat and orderly
— Be on time for meals
— Help your mother while he is away
— Pray for him often
— Write notes to him
— Bring him his coffee
— Give him hugs

A large portion of the ways a daughter can serve her father are indirect, like taking care of the little things that help the home run more smoothly, taking care of problems as they arise instead of waiting for him to fix them, and other such things. I remember one night I was washing the dishes and sweeping the kitchen floor, before heading to bed. My siblings were also completing their clean-up chores. After I finished my tasks, I looked down at the floor to see trash scattered about "on *my* clean floor"—obviously the sibling who had taken out the trash had left a mess! Irritated, I called for this sibling to come clean it up, only to find that he was already asleep in bed. Even further frustrated, I foolishly complained about it to my parents, who were working on some paperwork. Dad patiently offered to clean it up for me. Then, I saw the foolishness of my actions. This was such a minor inconvenience for me and it would not hurt me in the least to clean it up myself. I was perfectly capable of fixing this without making any fuss, yet, I had not been willing to take up the extra load without complaining. If I would have quietly done the job, my parents would have not been interrupted.

In situations like these, we daughters can correct things without being told, and without complaint. We can selflessly bear the load; we can die to self. These things will be a great blessing to our father, so he does not have to worry about trivial problems. By taking care of "little" issues, we also help our mother, in order for her to direct more of her energy and time assisting our dad.

One morning, my mom was sick in bed. As I took over her normal tasks, the Lord taught me some things. While I washed the breakfast dishes, I resolved to be patient and sweet to my siblings. After cleaning the kitchen, I did my devotions while the children were busy getting ready for school. I prayed for grace to be able to patiently keep my siblings quiet while Mom was resting.

For about an hour, things went well—until two of my siblings began giving me a hard time about their schoolwork. My patience started to wear down. I enjoy teaching them, but this morning I had to make sure they completed everything—I found they are quite accomplished at getting out of certain subjects when given a chance. By the end of the school session, I had given up my goal of staying cool and collected; I was simply trying to *survive*!

It was then that I realized maybe there is a reason why Mom gets frazzled at times. Frankly, I was beginning to wonder how she did it at all: I found so many things that needed tending to, for example:

- Making sure my brothers fed and watered the chickens, cows, pigs, turkeys, goats, and cared for the dog...what else?
- "Ahh! The clothes need to be taken out of the dryer..."
- "Oh! A milk customer was supposed to be here this morning, so I need to get the milk ready..."
- "What should I make for lunch?"
- "Oops! Today is Mom's ironing day. I need to iron the clothes from the past week..."

I was reminded once again how much energy is required to manage the household. I thank God for a mother who cares for our home so diligently, when she could simply hand over her responsibility to a government school and pursue other interests. Not only that, but she also faithfully provides us with nutritious meals, maintains a clean home, grows a garden, helps manage the family business, and more.

Stay-at-home mothers rarely have time for "extra" things; many tasks often get left behind between the more urgent day-to-day household duties. What can you do to lighten your mother's workload? Is it deep-cleaning the house once a week? helping her pick up clutter every night? making dinner? washing the dishes after meals? ironing the clothes? cleaning out that messy closet? sewing her a new dress? If you help with some of these tasks, she will be more free to catch up on other things which need to be done. Maybe all she needs is a bit of quiet time to plan and recollect while you tend to your siblings!

Being our mother's helper is practical preparation for the duties we will encounter as a mother and wife, Lord willing. Applying homemaking skills helps prepare us not only physically, but also mentally, for the transition of managing our own household someday. As we do these tasks we greatly assist our parents and lift their burdens.

Cheerful Sunshines

Our attitude as daughters has a great impact in our home. If we maintain a cheerful attitude, it will promote a loving and peaceful atmosphere, but if we are discontent and unhappy, it certainly will not be a blessing in our father's home. We must strive to consistently radiate the love, peace, and compassion of the Lord Jesus, though circumstances around us change daily. We, as believers, should trust in the unchanging Rock, and He is our eternal anchor. *"From the end of the earth will I cry unto thee, when my heart is overwhelmed: lead me to the rock that is higher than I"* (Psalm 61:2). Because of this refuge, we can maintain serenity and composure through Christ, no matter what vicissitudes may assail us. This unwavering attitude is a *choice* we face and a *choice* we must make.

As I washed the breakfast dishes one Saturday morning, I mentally planned out my day. Motivated to complete a project that day which I had been working on, I steadily scrubbed the dirty frying pan at hand. Suddenly, a change in my family's plans made what I wanted to accomplish impossible. With this change, I sullenly wondered what I would instead do with the morning. Even though this was a small inconvenience, at the time it seemed catastrophic to me—I was unhappy I could not do as planned.

If the Lord had not convicted me at that point and adjusted my attitude, I likely would have wasted the rest of the day; worse yet, my attitude would have hindered my family in their tasks. Yet, the Lord patiently pricked my heart, *You must learn to overcome little inconveniences like this. There is no reason to have a bad attitude because of a change in temporal plans. You should be following My plans, for they never change.* As I accepted this reality, immediately my spirit lifted and I thought, *Well, I should use my time wisely with a cheerful attitude no matter what happens, so here is a chance to overcome my emotions.*

As soon as I determined to not be discouraged over this situation—when I *chose* to have a good attitude—my emotions followed and I *felt* cheerful once again. Since I had made the choice to cheerfully accept the situation and focus on what the Lord wanted me to do, I was also available for my family if they needed my help. That day turned out well-spent, and I learned a very valuable lesson in the process.

Women are naturally emotional. I remember once a friend and I were sharing struggles we had experienced with our feelings. After a pause, I sighed, "Isn't it hard being a girl? We are so emotional!" Laughing, we both agreed. Praise the Lord, the story does not end here. Emotions are a blessing, when we place them under the control of Christ—not allow them to control us. Our God never changes, and we are commanded to imitate His likeness. Malachi 3:6 explains the unchanging character of our God, *"For I am the* LORD, *I change not."* We have a God Who is bigger than our emotions and bigger than our changing circumstances. Do we want to be the unstable, inconsistent person driven by the wind of changing circumstances, as described in James 1:6—*"He that wavereth is like a wave of the sea driven with the wind and tossed"?* We have a choice. We can choose to remain happy no matter what, with the Lord's help.

When we encounter times when we feel unhappy or discouraged, we should turn our feelings over to the Lord immediately—then make the conscious choice to trust God for the provision. *"Be careful for nothing; but in every thing by prayer and supplication with thanksgiving let your requests be made known unto God"* (Philippians 4:6). I may feel happy and cheerful one moment; the next minute, discouraged and grouchy. When my emotions change, I have found that it helps me to go to a quiet room, sit down, and dwell on the fact that Jesus is the same now as He was ten minutes ago. Not only that, but He also has not and never will change! Hebrew 13:8 gives this glorious promise, *"Jesus Christ the same yesterday, and today, and forever."* Then I pray the Lord would help me see the circumstances with clarity. It is so much better to do this than to allow my emotions make me feel depressed. If I will just stop and ask for God's grace to help me, He will do it.

We will be a great blessing in our home by maintaining a consistent attitude. When we make this commitment to be emotionally stable while trusting the Lord, it will have a major part in determining the entire family's spirit and will greatly influence our siblings' attitudes. We must learn to be master of daily discouragements; there will be greater hardships throughout our life. This is a critical choice we will make. Are we doing everything cheerfully, *"heartily, as to the Lord"* (Colossians 3:23)?

My friend Rachael fruitfully abides at home serving her family of seven. She shares about being a cheerful presence in her father's home, while supporting his vision of impacting the Church through hospitality, writing, and speaking.

"Surely we all agree that a happy girl is indeed a sweet sight to behold, but why? What is it about that radiant smile or the sublimely peaceful look emanating from her eyes that reveal that she is indeed happy, which makes us happy, too?

"A dear friend of mine seems to enjoy a constant peace and continually joyous attitude in all her circumstances. She is able to respond with patience and love. Could her enduring foundation of contentment, be the source of her consistent happiness? When I asked, my friend explained to me that she had chosen to not let her happiness depend on other people or on circumstances. Christ is indeed her Lord, as well as her Savior, and she knows that He is in control. With this in mind, she is able to be happy—she has made the decision to be. The results of her decision to trust and depend on God for everything, whether there is rain or sunshine in her life, has had as much of a profound effect on me as it has had on her own family. Could God do the same in my life?

"I had to first understand what happiness was. Noah Webster, in his 1828 Dictionary, described happiness as *'The agreeable sensations which spring from the enjoyment of good.'* Well, happiness is an emotion, this is true. It is also true that our emotions follow our thoughts and decisions. God's word clearly instructs us on how to think. *'Count it all joy in trials and tribulations.'* 'Count' means to choose, so we can choose to rest in the midst of any storm. Not only when there are sunny blue skies, but also when there are thunderstorms. Yet, how?

"How can our emotions respond in happiness when our circumstances are so difficult? I would like to share what I have learned. The key to being happy is found in our trust and submission to God. Once we have yielded our lives to His care, we must learn to think His thoughts! *'Be ye transformed by the renewing of your mind…Set your affections on things above…Whatsoever things be…true…honest… lovely…think on these things,'* and, *'Let the peace of God rule in your hearts.*' Knowing God's thought towards us is good, but if there is to be any real change, we must also put our trust into action, making right decisions in difficult times, with hope, patience, and contentment. Can you imagine how much more consistent our emotions could be if we did this daily? And how much more could we encourage and strengthen our family by simply demonstrating continual joy and happiness? Trusting God frees us to focus on others.

"As we grow in our reliance on God, we will realize our security only comes from His relationship to us. Consequently, we will become less dependent on things and people, and freer to serve others. My prayer is that we would be encouraged in our choice to focus on God, and our happy response to His loving faithfulness would blossom and spill over, bringing hope and encouragement to our family—and also to those friends and strangers around us who may yet be without His abiding peace and joy. Our happiness will be sweet for them to see!"

Making the Choice

Just as we have to choose what attitude we will harbor, we also have to choose to serve our authority even when we do not feel like doing so. While I want to honor my father, sometimes I do not *feel* the desire to do it. I wondered what was amiss and mentioned this to an older friend who is joyfully serving in her home. She replied,

"Don't worry about feelings—determine to serve cheerfully, and do it; your emotions will follow. Personally, when I serve my family, I do it because I love them—they are my most precious joy!"

Sisters, remember that our actions are a choice; we must discipline ourselves to do what is pleasing to the Lord. Do not worry about how you may feel about serving your father; just *do* it!

The Lord has also shown me I need to not only serve my father, but I must also *embrace* his vision as *my own*. It is not enough to indifferently accept his wishes. I must learn to take *delight* in his desires for our family. What my dad is excited about, I must notice and focus on. At times, this is difficult to do, but I am trying to learn to be passionate about my dad's vision; with God's grace, every daughter can do this. I believe when we have made the choice to make our father's vision first priority, it will in time become our own goal as well.

My dad has warned me that if a daughter cannot embrace her own father's vision, it is folly to believe she will embrace her future husband's vision—which by comparison, will be immature. The consequences become generational and eternal. Although learning to trust our father may seem difficult, this preparation is vital, because accepting our husband's choices may be even more difficult. Sometimes as girls, we think that after marriage everything will work out—"I'll love him!" Love is a choice, not a mushy emotion; submission is a choice, not some feeling we follow; honoring our authority is a choice, not a natural course of events. The choice is ours to make.

Examples in History

There are many examples in history of daughters who embraced their role as a supportive daughter. I enjoy reading about these girls; it is interesting to see how their choices impacted their world. My family has been reading recently about the Roosevelt families of past eras. Theodore Roosevelt's older sister, Bamie, had a spinal deformity, but she still sought to use her life to please her father. Though to others she may have been regarded as physically handicapped, to her father, she was *anything* but that in his home. I found this quote in *Mornings On Horseback* quite interesting,

> "Nothing pleased her [Bamie]...so much as pleasing [her father]... She would know how to manage, to take charge, and be everlastingly useful. The story among Roosevelts of later generations was that she

took over for her mother and ran the household from the time she was about fifteen, but this simply was not so. It was only that she *seemed* to be running everything, she was so capable and eager to cope."⁷

There are others who have not wisely used their influence as a daughter to honor their father. Another Roosevelt young lady, Theodore's own daughter Alice, was exactly the opposite: she used her father's fame for her own glory, and she did not support his influential position. Her negative example spurred other American girls in their natural rebellious spirits. What contrasted examples!

Let us be daughters who strengthen the very Kingdom of God through our lives of honor and devotion to His will in submitting to our authority. Let us persevere as we fulfill the role of a cornerpillar, and in so doing, impact *our* world for the glory of God.

on my shelf... RELATED RESOURCES

DVD:

— *The Return of the Daughters* by Anna Sofia & Elizabeth Botkin (Western Conservatory of Arts and Sciences; www.westernconservatory.org)

BOOKS:

— *Marriage to a Difficult Man: The Uncommon Union of Jonathan and Sarah Edwards* by Elisabeth Dodds (Audubon Press, P.O. Box 8055, Laurel, MS 39441, 800.405.3788; www.audubonpress.com)

— *Fathers & Daughters: Raising Polished Cornerstones* by David & Elysse Barrett (Widsom's Gate, P.O. Box 374, Covert, MI 49043; www.polishedcornerstones.com)

— *The Flower of the Family* by Mrs. Elizabeth Prentiss (A.B. Publishing Inc., 3039 S. Bagley, Ithaca, MI 48847)

a family daughter...
ELISHA A. WAHLQUIST

COMING AT THE END of a hectic week, that blessed day, Sunday, arrives. The Camden household is busy doing last-minute straightening, since church will meet at their spacious abode. Geneva assists her little sister dress, and then arranges the child's blond hair into twin buns festooned with ribbons. Mrs. Camden makes a last-minute walk through the house, checking to see that everything is in order. Another daughter, Abigail, goes over her lunch list to make sure everything is prepared. Abigail was in charge of all the meals this month, and she planned extra food for Sunday lunch so her father could invite others if he wished.

A shout from the younger ones by the front window—"Someone's here!"—sends everyone to the front door, where they warmly greet the first arrivals. There is a new family attending this morning, and each seeks to make them welcome. After the service, Mr. Camden invites the newcomers to stay for lunch. They accept, and the afternoon is filled with joyful fellowship. That evening, Mr. Camden thanks everyone, and Abigail in particular, for making it possible for them to invite over the new family for lunch. "That was wonderful," he says. "We got to know them better, and they felt truly welcome."

The ladies in this family were serving Mr. Camden and enabling his vision. Their family is a dynamic unit that has an enhanced impact because they are all working together towards the same goals.

Why do we serve those over us? Because 1) God has commanded it, and 2) we are thus serving Christ, our Savior and Lord. But our "masters" are not limited to a boss in the workplace, or even the government. There are various jurisdictions God has set up, and one of those is He has placed the parents in a place of responsibility over their children. *"Children, obey your parents in all things: for this is well pleasing unto the Lord"* (Colossians 3:20). In this article, I will focus mainly on serving our fathers, though there are many important ways we can serve our mothers, too.

How should we serve them? In Ephesians Paul says, *"Not with eyeservice, as menpleasers; but as the servants of Christ, doing the will of God from the heart; With good will doing service, as to the Lord, and not to men"* (6:6,7). We should serve those over us—our fathers—with industry, fidelity, conscientiousness, submission, and obedience. There is a very convicting verse in Luke which says, *"So likewise ye, when ye shall have done all those things which are commanded you, say, We are unprofitable servants: we have done that which was our duty to do"* (Luke 17:10). Do we serve our parents by doing only what they have asked us to do? Then we are unprofitable! *Strong's Concordance* suggests that another meaning for the word "unprofitable" here is "useless." Think of it—we are useless if we do not go beyond what is asked of us! This should inspire us to do more than is required, to use initiative to seek out ways we can serve and bless our authorities.

What are some practical ways daughters can serve their fathers? Just living at home, being alert to the needs there, and seeking out ways to help your father are big ways to serve him! Make it a habit to ask your father, "Dad, are there any projects or goals I can help you with?" Even if he cannot think of anything at the moment, you have demonstrated to him your willingness to assist, and he may think of something later. Be careful to listen to your dad's preferences, and be an enthusiastic part of making his dreams a reality. We can do much to encourage or discourage our father's ideas and plans by our reaction to them.

One of my father's goals has been to build our own debt-free house. At present, we are involved in doing just that, and it has been exciting to see ways we can aid him. My sister and I have spent hours on the computer looking up various building material options, discovering less toxic alternatives, and evaluating design ideas. This has saved him time, and helped further our building progress. Family work days also include projects such as wiring electrical circuits, digging trenches, and staining cement slab.

I know many girls across the country who are amazing assets to their fathers and families. Areas they serve include taking over the menu planning and meal preparation, aiding their father's political views by making calls, overseeing aspects of the family business, cheerfully investing in younger siblings, keeping the house clean to permit frequent hospitality, writing letters to family members, raising vegetable gardens, doing research, helping train siblings, orchestrating family ministry events, and creating money-saving projects and handiwork. These young women are vital elements in their home-life. You see, "serving our father" does not always mean that we are his secretary—although that certainly can be one way to serve. It involves a whole lot more!

One often-overlooked way that we can actively serve our father is by serving our mothers at home. Helping with the children is a major way to assist her. There are also many everyday tasks like cleaning, decluttering, and organizing that make our homes more pleasant, relaxing, and attractive to our fathers and set a tone of peace and orderliness in the house. If the house is usually in order, our fathers will feel freer to invite others over as well. Our homes are ultimately reflections upon him and our family.

Simply seeking to have every room neat before you leave it helps create a continual, pleasant home atmosphere. The small things, the "trifles" of life, are often the most important. Take the initiative to clean up—but do not expect others to necessarily notice; just do it all as service to God, looking to Him for your reward. Which brings us back to the point we made at the beginning of this article. All the "unimportant" tasks are important and meaningful when we focus on doing them unto the Lord. Can you think of many things more simple than giving someone a drink of water? That does not seem "spiritual" or important, but yet Jesus says, *"For whosoever shall give you a cup of water to drink in my name, because ye belong to Christ, verily I say unto you, he shall not lose his reward"* (Mark 9:41).

I once read a list of questions for wives to ask themselves. Several of them stood out to me as ones that are very useful for daughters to ask themselves, too. "Am I nurturing a spirit of loveliness in my home? Is there music in my voice? Is there sweetness on my countenance? Is there kindness on my lips?"

May God enable each one of us to be bright sunbeams of joyful service in our father's house!

ELISHA ANN WAHLQUIST *is a twenty-one-year-old homeschool graduate who seeks to delight in her femininity and in being her father's daughter. Investing in her five brothers and two sisters keeps her busy, but she still finds time to search the Scriptures, write, support her father's projects, and learn skills that, Lord willing, will be a blessing to a husband and children someday.*

"Likewise, ye younger, *submit yourselves* unto the elder.
Yea, all of you be **subject** one to another,
and be clothed with *humility*:
for God resisteth the *proud*,
and giveth *grace* to the **humble**."

[I PETER 5:5]

"Sweet stream, that winds through yonder glade,
Apt emblem of a **virtuous maid**—
Silent and chaste, she steals along,
Far from the world's gay, busy throng:
With *gentle* yet prevailing force,
Intent upon her destined course;
Graceful and useful all she does,
Blessing and blest where'er she goes;
Pure-bosom would as that watery glass,
And **heaven reflected** in her face."

[WILLIAM COWPER]

CHAPTER THREE

Our PARENTS' JOY

THE ONLY COMMANDMENT which is followed by a promise exhorts children,

> HONOR THY FATHER AND THY MOTHER
> *that thy days may be long upon the land*
> *which the Lord thy God has given thee.*[1]

We can see that this concept is incredibly important to God, for He promises great blessing upon those who honor their parents. Proverbs is also filled with promises to those that respect and heed their parents' counsel. *"My son...let thine heart keep my commandments: For length of days, and long life, and peace, shall they add to thee"* (3:1-2). In contrast, in the Bible, rebellious and disrespectful children are a sign of coming destruction. Proverbs 30:17 gives one clear warning: *"The eye that mocketh at his father, and despiseth to obey his mother, the ravens of the valley shall pick it out, and the young eagles shall eat it."* Romans 13:2 explains why our submission to authority is so vital, *"Whosoever therefore resisteth the power, resisteth the ordinance of God: and they that resist shall receive to themselves damnation."* The way we treat our parents ultimately reflects how we regard the Lord, which is obviously important.

God has been showing me how much my parents have sacrificed to raise a generation for His Kingdom. I am *so* thankful for my dad and mom; they have invested so much in my life. Everything I ever hope to be and anything I ever "accomplish" is thanks first to the Lord, and then to my parents' constant guidance. They have made me what I am! The Bible says that the crown of a son is his parents—*"for they shall be an ornament of grace unto thy head, and chains about thy neck"* (Proverbs 1:9).[2] Proverbs is a book of a father's advice to his son—a plea to heed the advice of your father.[3]

We are commanded to honor the position our parents have been given by God. It is important that we notice this command is not hinged upon what kind of parents we have—"If your dad and mom are nice, or if they are godly, then you should honor them." It is a *command*. Some girls have said, "But you don't know my dad [or mom]. He is so insensitive and does not understand my feelings. He doesn't know how to relate to me! I do not feel honor toward him." Our feelings or opinions do not have a vote. If a daughter is struggling to show her father or mother honor which she does not feel, she needs to make the choice to honor them anyway. I would challenge her to set a goal to show honor in their strained relationship for a week—to go out of her way to show her father and mother appreciation, to talk with them, to thank them, to do whatever she can to honor them—and see the change her honor made in their relationship. This honor should be shown all the time. *Our* repentance of heart is a key—we cannot wait for our parents to come to us to heal a strained relationship if we are not ready to go to them in repentance, ready to honor them just as they are. Every daughter must make the choice to honor her parents, though she clearly sees their faults. Parents are not perfect, just as no daughter is perfect. We need to learn to be graceful toward their weaknesses, and instead of criticizing them for these areas, pray for them and focus on their strengths.

It is vital that we realize we must honor our parents as our God-appointed authority; it has nothing to do with whether they deserve it or not.[4] I want to stress this because we need to realize that our future mate, who will be our authority, *will* fail too; every one who marries will marry a sinner. Our husband will not be perfect! He may make foolish decisions at times, and he will likely be our peer in age and maturity. We may not *feel* like giving him respect at times, but we will be required to honor his position as our God-given authority. We must make a conscious choice to honor our parents, so that as wives, we also will make the right decision to honor our husband.

God-honoring love chooses to honor, regardless of circumstances, faults, or feelings. I encourage you to ponder the verses in I Corinthians 13. The more I read this description, the more I am challenged to display true love—which is selfless, humble, patient, pure, trusting, enduring, and kind. This is a far cry from the picture our bankrupt society has portrayed of love. True, Christ-like, selfless love gives—not takes. Do not develop a false idea and expectation of love.

> "Charity suffereth long, and is kind; charity envieth not; charity vaunteth not itself, is not puffed up, doth not behave itself unseemly, seeketh not her own, is not easily provoked… Charity never faileth."[5]

Ways to Bless

Honor means "to revere; to respect; to treat with deference and submission."[6] When we show respect for our parents, we please God.[7] Though I have much room to grow in this area, I want to share some of the ways God has shown me that I need to honor to my parents. Let us press on in this journey together!

The attitude we have toward our parents is very important. Our honor should be such that we always respect them—especially when their backs are turned. *"Let them learn first to shew piety at home, and to requite their parents: for that is good and acceptable before God"* (I Timothy 5:4). God sees our heart even if our parents do not, and this also sets an example for our siblings, who watch us closely. Our brothers and sisters watch to see if "big sister obeys Mom" when Mom is not around; they want to see our attitude when our parents are not watching. We may not realize how much the way we regard our parents affects our siblings' attitude as well. I have learned how important my responses are as an example to my siblings—if I make even one disrespectful expression or word to my parents, my brothers and sister immediately pick up on it. If they see me do this even one time, no matter how many times I tell them they shouldn't do it, it is like "permission" for them to follow suit. On the other hand, when I *consistently* "practice what I preach," they have no backing, "You did it last month!"

When we speak of our parents, our tone of voice and words communicate a lot about our attitude toward them. Praise your mom and dad. Also, do not interrupt them when they are talking to someone, and be careful not to correct them during their conversations unless it is very important. No matter how well-intentioned, this can be disrespectful, and I Peter 5:5 commands the younger to *"submit yourselves unto the elder...and be clothed with humility."* Once, we ate dinner with a family we know, and as our parents talked, their teenage daughter constantly interrupted her parents, correcting them on minor points. It was dishonoring to her parents, and it was very distracting to follow their conversation amidst her comments. While supporting what they are saying, let your parents be the conversationalist—unless, of course, they specifically include you.

Prayer is a wonderful way to support and bless our parents. Such a simple thing as prayer can make a huge difference in our homes. Parents carry such a big responsibility in raising a family. Especially when my dad or mom is facing a difficult situation, I try to ask the Lord to grant strength, patience, and wisdom to them. What a pillar of blessing and strength we can become if we lift up our family daily *"unto the throne of grace...and find grace to help in time of need"* (Hebrews 4:16).

I have also seen the importance of us daughters respecting the wishes of other parents. Recently we visited a family who we had not seen for several years, and my friends invited me to their bedroom after dinner so we could talk together. When I replied that my parents do not usually want me to do this, they immediately said, "Ok, that's fine! Let's visit in the living room." What a blessing it was to be around friends who respected my parents' authority. On the other hand, I know other girls who, when I have said this, have replied in repulsive tones, "Why will your parents not allow you to do that? See, we cannot even talk in here because everyone else is too loud. We're wasting the time you have here to catch up!" The remainder of our visit is unpleasant because of their disrespect for my parents' wishes.

Embracing Correction

Another way to display honor is by accepting our parents' correction and advice. The Bible says one key difference between a fool and a wise man is their response to correction. A fool will reject correction; in contrast, a wise man will realize his need and gratefully embrace correction. Proverbs repeatedly warns of this defining factor:

"Correction is grievous unto him that forsaketh the way: and he that hateth reproof shall die." (Proverbs 15:10)

"A reproof entereth more into a wise man than a hundred stripes into a fool." (Proverbs 17:10)

If you have beheld someone humbly receive correction, it must remain a vivid memory in your mind. I have been especially blessed by one friend's example in this area. Last year, while spending time in her family's home, she exemplified a wise daughter when corrected by her mother. She accepted it, apologized, and cheerfully went on. When I mentioned this to her later, she admitted, "Honestly, I hate correction!" She continued, "But God has worked in my heart so much this past year; I have realized how much I need to be shown my faults. I have struggled and often have failed, but Jesus has been faithful to help me respond humbly." When she surrenders to God her feelings, He gives grace to overcome her flesh. She is still learning to overcome pride, yet her example has greatly encouraged me to accept correction with a humble heart.

When I am corrected or given instruction, my natural reaction is to defend myself, but the Lord wants me to turn from my selfish desires. It is a difficult battle and requires constant guarding of the heart and mouth, but God will extend grace and strength to us, so that *"in all these things we are more than conquerors through him that loved us"* (Romans 8:37). If I foolishly reject correction, I am also spurning the blessings of God that come with humility. *"He that shall humble himself shall be exalted"* (Matthew 23:12). Let us be ready to accept our parents' correction, which we so desperately need.

The Intent

Outwardly complying with our parents while inwardly grumbling is not true obedience. We should obey with our *heart*. If we truly honor our parents in our heart, outward obedience will be a joy. God knows our hearts—*"the eyes of the Lord are in every place, beholding the evil and the good,"* Proverbs 15:3 warns. We need to repent when we fail to show this honor that the Lord requires.

I have learned that showing my parents honor goes farther than just obeying their "commands"—it is also respecting their wishes and intent. We probably know what our parents' preferences are, so we must not only *obey* their requests, but also *honor* their preferences and desire.

As I entered my teenage years, I keenly felt the difference between the standards of my family and others. It seemed everyone I knew was allowed to do something my parents would not permit me to do or wear something that my parents did not want me to wear. I wanted to be *like* someone—especially girls who were older than me.[9] I often struggled with this, and even tested their rules at times! I look back now with thankfulness for their firm requirements, and am glad that they did not give in to my desires.

After a few years, these differences did not seem to pressure me as much; I was content with my parents' standards. Just when I thought I had overcome this weakness, my Dad told us ladies that he preferred us to wear our hair a certain way at church. I complied, though unwillingly. Several months later the Lord showed me my sinful attitude toward my dad's wishes. While traveling out of town, we visited a new church, and I chose to wear my hair differently. Dad did not say anything about it at the time—but later, he made a reference to my decision. That was quite an eye-opener for me as I realized I was once again going against my parent's wishes. Even if my dad did not *require* it, I knew what he preferred so I should do it *out of honor*. I am continually learning this lesson.

> "*Obedience* must be from the heart, and yet obedience must not be restricted to the heart."[8]
> —Dr. Greg L. Bahnsen

I am very grateful that my parents have not compromised on their standards. Knowing I have these boundaries actually gives me freedom—and that protection makes life easy! I have also learned as I am found faithful with the privileges my parents *have* granted, the more freedom they give me as I mature. A spirit of honor asks, "What would my parents prefer me to do in this situation?" rather than an ever-undermining attitude of, "What can I get by with this time?" Of course, this does not mean I do not struggle with the pressures of conformity, because I do—and many other girls I have talked to admit that this is an area in which they also struggle. Do not feel alone in this battle! You may feel pressures, but remember that the Lord will help you overcome these temptations, and will bless your steadfast honor. I encourage you to honor your parents, even if what they want you to do is unpopular.

There have been countless situations when my parents have suggested something I did not want to do, but when I obey, I have witnessed God's blessings. For example, several years ago when I began music lessons, I found some of the other students to be unfriendly. At my parents' encouragement, I strived to show myself uncompetitive, making a point to compliment their performances. I received no positive responses; thus, I became discouraged after several months. The very night at a recital when I gave up my efforts, Dad hinted, "Did you tell 'so and so' that she did a good job tonight?" I really did not *want* to do this when I had been turned down so many times, but at his suggestion, I congratulated my fellow student. At the next recital, I performed a piece which had taken me many months to learn and memorize. This same student came to me and shocked me by saying, "You did a great job!" I was so blessed when I least expected it.

There have been times when my parents have advised me not to pursue certain friendships, or participate in certain events, or spend time around some people, because they did not think these situations would be good influences in my life. I can look back and see how right their advice was, and I thank the Lord for their protection.

Trustworthy

A friend once said to me, "How it pains our parents' hearts if we are not totally open before them!" We must be forthright in every area of life with our parents. If we are deceptive, we can be sure our sin will be found out, as Numbers 32:23 warns: *"Ye have sinned against the Lord: and be sure your sin will find you out."* How true I have found this verse to be. It *never* pays to be deceptive! This is not only a sin against our parents, but also a transgression against God—He abhors the lying tongue. Proverbs 12:22 points out, *"Lying lips are abomination to the Lord: but they that deal truly are his delight."* We cannot draw close to the Lord when we trying to hide our sin—when *"we say that we have fellowship with him, and walk in darkness, we lie, and do not the truth"* (I John 1:6). He sees every sin in our heart and when we try to hide this from Him, our fellowship with Him will be hindered. If there is something on your heart right now that you are struggling with, do not wait another minute. Please share it with your mom and dad—confess your sin to them and the Lord. It may be hard, but the rewards of being open and honest are abundant. Let us delight in truth, being trusted in the sight of God and man, like the virtuous woman: *"The heart of her husband doth safely trust in her, so that he shall have no need of spoil"* (Proverbs 31:11).

We should make our parents our best friends and trusted confidants. Ask your parents for their input in various situations; seek their thoughts in even minor decisions. I encourage you to go to your parents with every area of life. Learn to share your heart with your parents and confide in them your deepest dreams and feelings. Although it has been a struggle for me to open my heart in some areas, the Lord has been teaching me the blessings of confiding in my parents. I want them to know my feelings, but to develop that relationship, I must be willing to open my heart with them. When I have shared my struggles, the results have been *so* worth the effort. My parents are glad to have me share, and I am always blessed by their advice. When situations are utterly confusing to me, my parents can give me a clearer view. There are things that I cannot and should not carry alone; my parents are there to lead and help me through these issues.

We do not need to wait for our parents to come and ask us to share what is on our heart. We need to *seek* them out, seek their confidence, seek their counsel. Deuteronomy 32:7 says, *"Remember the days of old, consider the years of many generations: ask thy father, and he will show thee; thy elders, and they will tell thee."* I know it can be hard to take initiative to do this, but our parents do not always know when we are struggling if we have not done our part in sharing it with them! How can they offer godly advice if we have not confided in them and asked for guidance? Showing you desire your dad and mom's input and that you delight in their counsel will bless them and also strengthen your relationship. We must do whatever is necessary to develop ongoing communication. Candace Joy, the eldest daughter in a family of sixteen, lives at home with her parents and siblings. She shares what a blessing it has been in her life to maintain open communication with her parents.

"WHEN A YOUNG LADY takes time to build a relationship with her parents through communication, she shows them honor. Communication is a vital ingredient to every good relationship, and our relationship with our parents is no exception.

"Communication is a two-way street. If you want a strong relationship with your parents, you will need to put forth effort. Take the time to converse with your dad and mom; look for or make opportunities to share your heart with your parents.

"Taking time to talk is a good start, but there is something else that you can do to make the time when you talk together meaningful and productive—be open. Tell them about your dreams, your struggles, conversations with your friends, what is going on in your spiritual life, and things that are concerning you. Ask your parents for specific counsel and ask them to pray for areas you are struggling with, or decisions you are facing. Asking for counsel and then obeying your parents' counsel shows that you value your parents' opinion. If you are wondering how you should act in a certain situation, ask your parents. They have a lot of wisdom that they can share with you.

"God has greatly blessed my life through communicating with my parents. They have listened to me when I have needed someone to talk to, given me godly counsel, and prayed for areas that I am concerned, struggling, and or uncertain about. I would encourage you to ask the Lord to show you areas that you have dishonored your parents and then repent of those things. Look to Him for strength throughout the day as you strive to obey Him by honoring your parents."

In the everyday schedule of life, it can be hard to find time to talk about subjects in depth, but we must make it a priority. The method that works best in every relationship varies, but the key is *keeping your heart open.* You can write letters to your parents, keep a journal together—share questions, quotes, insights, exchange ideas, and glean from their experiences. Sometimes it is helpful for me to regularly write notes to my parents, sharing struggles and questions.

> "*Seek their counsel,* ask questions, glean from their wisdom of years, be grateful for the things they share. Do not ask unless you really want to know; then apply what you learn. Love them—they are...sacrificing their own time, emotional and physical energy for you. So be glad for the Lord's work in you through them."
>
> —Rebecca (28), Daughter at Home

Someday we will not have our parents with us everyday; one day the Lord will call them Home. Do all you can to learn from their wisdom—ask them things like the date they were saved, what their favorite Scripture is, about their growing-up years. They can share inestimable wisdom from their hindsight perspective. What would they do differently in their life as they look back? Not only will you learn much good advice, but you will also preserve your heritage. These records will become a wonderful keepsake to you and your future generations.

I took a Christian business class a few years ago. I think one of the most beneficial lessons I gleaned from the entire course was from one assignment, which was to have my parents write my five major character weaknesses and strengths. I also was to write a list evaluating myself, and then we compared notes. When my mom and dad each showed me their lists I was quite surprised; I did not realize I had many of the weaknesses they pointed out. It was amazing to see myself in someone else's light. I become blind to so many of the faults that others can see clearly in my life. This exercise also blessed our relationship because we began to understand one another's unique personality and character differences. It helped me appreciate the different gifts each of my family members has been given. I highly recommend you and your parents do this evaluation together!

A Testimony

One young lady shares that investing in her relationship with her mother has been worth the effort:

"A CLOSE mother/daughter relationship does not just 'happen.' It must be cultivated daily. A daughter must be willing to forsake her pride and draw close to her mother by confiding temptations and struggles, and making a conscious effort of her will to delight in and look up to her mother. This can be difficult—but some of the best things come through patient struggles and investment.

"In my own life, I have found that confessing thoughts, struggles and temptations to my mother are 'giants'—but whenever I have asked God to give me the strength to tell them to my mother, He has been faithful to give me the needed strength. It is impossible to explain the freedom, understanding, and close-knit joy I have experienced whenever I have taken my struggles to my mother and sought her insight and wisdom. Even in little things, seeking and asking your mother's advice and trying to follow it builds the mother and daughter bond. Your mother has gone through many of the same struggles you have, and she will have a wealth of wisdom to share. I have often gained deeper insight for situations by discussing them with my mother and asking, 'What do you think I should do?' or 'How should I respond in this certain situation?' Sharing and talking about small issues as well as big ones will help your mother become your best friend. Be eager to spend time with your mother. If she's going to take a walk or run some errands and asks if anyone is interested in going, eagerly jump on the chance to be with her. When she senses your delight in spending time with her, it will really boost your relationship. When we make an effort with our will to delight our mothers, our emotions will follow, and we will begin to delight in them!

"The road ahead may be a hard one as you strive to build a deeper mother/daughter relationship. But it is well worth it. My dear mother has become a best friend to me, and I would not trade her relationship for any number of outside friends!"

The Promise

The decisions we make today will affect our posterity. In Genesis 3:6, Eve made a very detrimental decision which impacted all future seed. Noah, Abraham, and other great patriarchs also made choices that still affect our world today. We also face decisions that will affect *our* future generations—it starts in everyday areas like honoring our parents, which is very important in the sight of God.

God will bless our efforts to honor our parents. This is part of the fulfillment of the promise that comes with the sixth commandment: *"That thy days may be long."* This may not necessarily mean that we as individuals will live long, though God may possibly determine our days according to our actions. This verse is a promise that our Christian lineage will continue in God's blessing. Don't you desire that in a hundred years, if the Lord tarries, thousands of your descendants will be faithfully spreading the message of the salvation of Christ? Let us remain faithful and make the right choices every day to honor our parents. Do not give up in well-doing; you will reap a great and rewarding harvest!

This is a decision that will decide our children's future.

RELATED RESOURCES

AUDIO:

– *God's Way to Deal With Your Wrong Emotions* by Dr. S. M. Davis (Solve Family Problems, Lincoln, IL 62656, 800.500.8853; *www.solvefamilyproblems.com*)

– *The Woman's Role in the Home* by Mrs. Marge Barth (Barth Family Ministries, 339 Parkhill Road, Cornwall, VT 05753; 802.462.2001)

– *Victory for Daughters: Home Schooled Daughters Speak Out About Virtue, Serving Their Fathers, and the Noble Call of Womanhood* by Kelly Brown and Sarah, Rebekah, & Hannah Zes (The Vision Forum Inc., 800.440.0022)

BOOKS:

– *Letters on Practical Subjects to a Daughter* by Mr. William B. Sprague (Grace and Truth Books, 3406 Summit Boulevard, Sand Springs, Oklahoma 74063, 918.245.1500; *www.graceandtruthbooks.com*)

– *Mother* by Kathleen Norris

– *Coming in on a Wing and a Prayer* by Kelly (Brown) Bradrick

– *Feminine By Design* by Mr. Scott Brown (above three books available through The Vision Forum Inc., 4719 Blanco Road, San Antonio, TX 78212; *www.visionforum.com*)

a family daughter...
TIFFANY M. SCHLICHTER

MY PARENTS ARE MY heroes and I love them beyond words. Over the years, I have become more aware of the countless sacrifices they make for me. As I have pondered their constant self-denial, unfailing love, godly counsel, and wise guidance, I realize that they deserve my utmost respect, love, gratitude, and honor.

Being their delightful daughter, however, has been an ongoing journey. When I was very young, obedience was expected, so it quickly became a way of life for me, but I soon found it possible to obey my mom and dad without honoring them. Yet through the Lord's ever faithfulness, I can attest to the joys and rich blessings of honoring my parents with my heart and actions. One passage of Scripture that has become a treasure to me is Proverbs 1:7–9: *"The fear of the Lord is the beginning of knowledge: but fools despise wisdom and instruction. My son, hear the instruction of thy father, and forsake not the law of thy mother. For they shall be an ornament of grace unto thy head, and chains about thy neck."* I find that when I seek to honor my parents—outwardly and in my heart—it is much easier for me to obey them, to accept their leadership, and to trust their decisions.

One thing that comes to mind is what Jesus said in John 14:15: *"If ye love Me, keep My commandments."* The same has been true of my relationship with my parents. In desiring to love and honor them, I have learned to take seriously the standards and guidelines they have set for me. Their restrictions are physical and spiritual protections, and though there were times when I did not necessarily feel excited about it, I have made efforts to express my gratitude to my mom and dad for their protection over me. I have also noticed that when I am away from them, whether by myself or alone with friends, it is critical that I honor their wishes and "keep their commandments" by upholding the standards and restrictions they have set for our family. When I was younger, I sometimes wondered why I was not allowed more freedom. Looking back, however, I see that the more I have trusted and honored my parents, the more freedom and independence they have granted me. As I have grown in years and wisdom, my mom and dad have allowed me to make increasingly more of my own decisions. When given these opportunities, I try to choose the way that honor the Lord and my parents. As a result, they place greater confidence in my judgment.

Trusting my parents has been an important lesson to learn, since some of the decisions they make for our family set us apart from others. Though I realized they were following the Lord's will to be different than the world, it would occasionally frustrate me when their choices made me different than my "likeminded" friends. The Lord showed me that I was dealing with pride and fear of man. Endeavoring to walk humbly before God and to live for Christ alone has helped me to learn contentment in trusting my parents' choices. It also gives me a greater delight in how the Lord leads our family. *"In the fear of the LORD is strong confidence: and His children shall have a place of refuge. The fear of the LORD is a fountain of life, to depart from the snares of death"* (Proverbs 14:26–27).

I truly believe that God uses our parents as crucial instruments to prepare us for the next season of being under the authority and leadership of a husband. It has been said that a good daughter will make a good wife. I still have areas to improve in the way of honoring my parents, and am working toward being a godlier, more faithful, and more delightful daughter to them and to the Lord.

We will never regret the time and energy we invest into honoring, serving, and loving our parents, because God promises blessings to those who obey and follow His will in every aspect of life!

> "Be not deceived; God is not mocked:
> for whatsoever a man **soweth**, that *shall he also reap*.
> For he that soweth to his flesh
> shall of the flesh reap corruption;
> but he that soweth to the *Spirit*
> shall of the Spirit reap life everlasting.
> And let us not be weary in well doing: for in due season
> *we shall reap, if we faint not.*"
> —GALATIANS 6:7–9

TIFFANY M. SCHLICHTER graduated from homeschool high school in 2007 and resides in Montgomery, Texas, with her parents, six brothers, and sister. A free-lance author from her home, Tiffany has written and published three books, and also publishes a monthly magazine. She finds great joy in encouraging fellow Christian daughters in the ways of their Savior.

"The servant of the Lord
must not strive; but be gentle unto all men, apt to teach, patient,
In meekness instructing those that oppose themselves;
if God peradventure will give them repentance
to the acknowledging of the truth."

[II TIMOTHY 2:24-5]

"Make us masters of ourselves,
that we may be the servants of others."

[SIR ALEXANDER PATERSON]

CHAPTER FOUR

The FAMILY SISTER

S MY FAMILY will attest, when I was younger, I was much more active outdoors. I have fond memories of my brother and I climbing trees, tromping in the woods on rainy days, and riding our bikes around in circles for hours in our driveway. On sunny summer afternoons, we would draw chalk "roads" on the driveway, complete with chalk-writing stop signs, red lights, and a gas station—constructed from a brick wall and garden hose.

It has been a while since I have joined in these activities. Recently, Samuel begged me to come outside and ride bikes with him. At first, I brushed him off. *I need to work on a project...I need to practice music....I have clothes to fold....I want to write that letter...* I had plenty of excuses. Of course, he paid no heed to any of them. His emphatic solution was "Do it later!" With persistence on his part, I conceded to play with him and to show him how to draw bike roads.

It was well worth it. My siblings loved having me join them and showing them things I did in those days when I "was a kid," as they say.

Samuel was right; the things I thought I needed to do could be done later. Eternal investments cannot wait; the opportunity will be forever lost if not captured. Spending time with my siblings and investing in them is much more profitable than many other things I can do.

By investing in my siblings, I can impact the very Kingdom of God by influencing another life for the Lord. Encouraging our siblings to seek the Lord also honors our parents as they seek to raise a godly heritage. Our influence is especially potent in the lives of our younger siblings—they watch us and will probably follow in our footsteps.

If we invest in these sibling relationships during the days God has given us together, what a blessing this foundation will prove to be for the rest of our lives. Proverbs 17:17 says, *"A friend loveth at all times, and a brother is born for adversity."* My mom testifies, "When you are adults, these firmly-founded sibling relationships will be of the utmost importance."

Best Friends

When I was younger, I had few friends, though I often prayed for someone with whom I could fellowship. Looking back, I am now grateful the Lord saw fit to wait in answering my prayer, because during those formative years He had me spend the majority of my time with my family rather than with outside influences. I am incredibly grateful for each friend God has blessed me with today, yet I believe that growing up without many "friends" has helped me learn to make my family my closest friends, and to better balance my priorities and time now.

Several years ago, the Lord provided fellowship which was a blessing to me in that particular season. Later, God led us away from that source and I felt terribly lonely. It was hard for me to adjust to having no "outside" friends again. My journal around this time gives an idea of the struggle I experienced:

CHAPTER FOUR — *The Family Sister*

"I am feeling rather insecure and hopeless...things my heart has become based and focused on are crumbling. I realize God may be keeping me from this until I can learn to place Him first in my heart. It is hard not to place the things of the world in the place that only God can fill. Teach me, Lord! May this desert become the time of abundance in You."

A few months after this was penned, I realized,

"I pleaded with God for years to help me grow in Him, to give me freedom in Him. Then when He did, I screamed out in pain, 'No God!' This painful experience was really the answer to all my prayers—a blessing in disguise. I am so grateful He does not grant all our requests and that He loves us enough to teach valuable lessons."

As I look back, I can testify that taking me through this trial *was* the best thing the Lord could have taken me through, because I had shifted my focus from my family—my priority—to other friends. Through these situations, He has shown me that my family members should and can be my very best and closest friends, aside from Jesus. They are always with me, thus, provide security for me as well.

Maybe to you, the idea of making your *family* members your best *friends* sounds unfulfilling, boring, or impossible. I used to have this attitude too—I have cried from the depths of my heart for fulfillment in a friend. But where I was searching for it was exactly where I was *not* going to find it! God *"setteth the solitary in families"* (Psalm 68:6)—what a beautiful gift. While godly, Christ-focused friendships are a great blessing, they are not mandatory in every stage of life. Learn to invest in your siblings and parents. Make them your priority. Have you ever thought, *I really need a friend who is likeminded, with whom I can share my heart?* I can tell you that you are living with them—your parents already know you and can offer the encouragement you need, and your siblings can be your best friends. God may take you through a "solitary" time so you will "meet" your own family. This is a blessing!

I can honestly say that I love being with my family; they really are my closest friends. I love being around my siblings. We look forward to sharing our news with each other when we have been separated for even a short time. We often give each other a nod or look that only we can interpret—we oftentimes know what each other is thinking, because we know each other so well! Of course, we are still growing in these relationships and are not perfect, by any means. We face issues every day, yet by God's grace, each skirmish serves to knit our family closer together as a cohesive unit.

Of True Importance

We must establish godly priorities so we do not place our personal interests over these important family relationships. It is vital that we prioritize our activities so we put our family first in life. Fourteen-year-old Angela Masloske, second-born in a family of seven children, shares what the Lord has taught her about priorities:

> THE LORD HAS BEEN clearly showing me how to use my time in a much wiser way. He has lead me to give up a certain interest of mine that I enjoyed—blogging. I had started a blog last year with my parents' approval and loved writing posts or responding to comments.
>
> "But one night, the Lord showed me a glimpse of His will about my blog when my little brother Andrew asked me what I was going to do one night. I responded that I was going to be spending time with him, and his whole countenance lit up as he asked if I was sure I was not going to blog. That just crushed my heart. My seven-year-old brother thought blogging was more important to me than him!
>
> "I felt the Lord prompting me to stop blogging because it took so much time away from my family. One day a few weeks later when I was still questioning the wisdom of keeping my blog, I received

CHAPTER FOUR — *The Family Sister*

an email from a friend, who encouraged me to delete my blog. This reassured me that Andrew's response must be a sign from the Holy Spirit; I wholeheartedly agreed.

"That night I wrote my last blog post sharing my story and informing my readers that I would delete my blog. After I clicked the 'publish post' tab, I felt like a shackle had been removed! That night I wrote in my journal, 'I have only felt one thing all evening—freedom. I gave up my blog today and I feel like a new person. Now I can be with my family more.'

"I have not regretted my decision even once after it was made and I have been able to spend much more time with family, and learn more skills that will help me in the future.

"Honoring the Lord in this decision has brought happiness, freedom, and joy. Through this situation I have learned that when you simply dedicate something to the Lord and fully trust in Him, He will use it for good as He promises in Romans 8:28: *'All things work together for good to them that love God.'* Sisters, strive to serve Him with your whole heart and always give what He asks of you, no matter what the cost!"

> *"One of the most important* ways we can set an example is by spending time with God. One night my older brother got out his Bible and started reading it after our two younger siblings were in bed. Because of his example, I laid aside what I was doing and read my Bible, too. Night after night, I continued to read my Bible because of his example. Setting a good example for our siblings can be so powerful."
>
> —Maggie Bullington (15)

We need to make sure that every activity we are involved in is God's will for us, and it benefits our family members. If something takes excessive time away from our family and occupies our minds constantly, we should reevaluate these things. We need to clear our days of unprofitable projects and time-wasters.

Serving

Jesus Himself was a servant of mankind, and He stopped to bless even the little children. *"But Jesus said, Suffer little children, and forbid them not, to come unto me"* (Matthew 19:14). It is easy for me to get in the habit of thinking my younger siblings are there to help me. Just as I rebuke them for not doing something I ask, God reminds me I should instead be serving *them*! Jesus stooped to *serve* depraved men, instead of demanding their service and dedication. So I need to set an example that glorifies the Lord through humble service to my siblings.

Do my siblings think of me as the lazy older sister with no initiative to help, who demands service of them, who criticizes their faults; who, in short, is someone they would rather not be around? On the other hand, do my they regard me as a gentle, caring, helpful sister who encourages them to become more like Jesus and grow in character?

As we treat our siblings with grateful humility, this will be a great blessing to the entire family. My brother Jonathan displays a thankful attitude. Often, he will come up to Mom and thank her for dinner. He remembers to thank me when I clean out the dishwasher for him. His example often inspires me to reach out in thoughtfulness to my family.

Caring

SITTING IN FRONT OF A WINDOW in her favorite chair, Lily's pen briskly glided over the paper. Sunlight streamed in onto Lily's stationery as she related her family's latest news to her best pen-pal. As she wrote, her little brother came stomping in from his play and ran over to Lily, breaking the peaceful silence. "Lily, I made the biggest tree fort! Come look and see it!" Lily looked up from her paper, still deep in thought, and brushed Johnny aside, "I'm busy. Don't interrupt! I lost my train of thought. I'll be out later." With a little more persuasion, Johnny disappointedly leaves the room.

CHAPTER FOUR — *The Family Sister*

Be assured, this little brother will not come many more times to tell "big sister" about his news... she will never become his confident if she continues to ignore his cares.

———

As Sue chatted with some friends, she kept a close eye on her little siblings who romped about in the grass. Occasionally, her little two-year-old brother waved his sand shovel, looking over at his big sis. She cheerfully called, "What do you have there?!" as he giggled. Joining in the conversation again with her friends, she added some input, all the while watching her little charges. As her friend, Flossie, showed her some pictures from a recent trip, Sue noticed her little sister fall from the swing. "Oh," she jumped up, "Are you ok?" she called as she rushed to the rescue. "Ouch! My finger!" little Bekah whimpered, looking fearfully at the blood on her finger. "Oh no, let me see. Let's fix it up with a band-aid," Sue comforted. As she headed inside with Bekah, she called over to her friends, "I'll be back in a bit!"

As I have witnessed these two contrasting scenes, the Lord convicted me that I need to show more love and concern for my siblings. I need take time to listen to their news and latest projects, and interact with them when they come to tell me something they are doing. It can be easy not to give my siblings my full attention when they are talking to me. The Lord has shown me how important it is to stop what I am doing, look them in the eyes, listen to them, and answer them. We should take time to play with our little sisters' new baby doll or our brothers' latest Lego® truck invention. We should not only listen, but also *interact*—even if we know nothing about building cool Lego® trucks!

One of my friends told me when her brother arrived home from work, her siblings rushed to the door and pounced on him, telling their latest "exciting" news. That made me think. Honestly, is being bombarded with a confusion of excited chatter what you want to walk into after a long day of work? But his siblings knew he would care about what they had to say; they knew he was excited to see them after being separated. Do our siblings know we care and will patiently listen? I certainly want to grow in this area!

Too often siblings relationships involve foolishness and light-heartedness. As sisters, we must show genuine interest in the *spiritual* state of our siblings. Our siblings should know we are concerned about their state before God, and we must seek to spiritually invest in their lives through prayer, encouragement, concern, and setting a good example. When we encourage siblings to read their Bible daily or read it with them, teach them musical instruments, sing together, or other activities, it has a great impact. When our siblings are facing difficulties, we must listen and pay attention with our mind, eyes, and heart.

Gentle Kindness

We were enjoying fellowship with two sweet families. I was in the kitchen talking with Rebecca, the oldest of nine children. I have so much to learn from older daughters, so I was thrilled to hear her share about her journey of family relationships and contentment. Our parents were in the living room involved in a lively discussion, and other adult children were likewise profitably conversing around the home. Outdoors, our younger siblings were involved in a game of tag.

As Rebecca and I conversed, muffled sobs from outdoors drifted in through the open window. I did not notice, but as soon as Rebecca heard, her eyes widened and she rushed outside. She found her nine-year-old brother had fallen from a tree limb and bumped his head. Rebecca gently led him to the sink to wash his scrapes and asked him what happened, setting things right once more. Soon, he was again outside playing with the others as if nothing occurred. Our parents' conversation was not disturbed since Rebecca took care of him.

CHAPTER FOUR — *The Family Sister*

Rebecca's gentle and caring spirit spoke to me. As I pondered what my reaction would have been if it had been my own brother, I realized that I am not overly caring. Even though her brother was not badly hurt, Rebecca still stopped what she was doing and made a point to notice. She was investing in his life. I can only wonder how her little brother will lovingly remember his big sister as he grows up.

Gentleness is something that is beautiful for a young lady to model, and God requires His children to emulate this; II Timothy 2:24 says, *"The servant of the Lord must...be gentle."* Our siblings will have more respect for us if we are a sister of meek gentleness. I want to be the sister who loves, cares, and encourages my siblings—someone they can come to and share their struggles.

Protecting

My older brother's chore used to be to take out our trash every night. I thought my big brother was great—because no matter what I did to him, he always seemed to be invincible. He was so patient! I am no exception to the mischievous streak that runs in our family, so occasionally, I would sneak outside before he took the trash out at night and hide under or beside the trash cans. As he rounded the corner of the house, I would jump out of my hiding place and scare him. When this chore was passed down to one of my younger brothers, I thought it would be really fun to scare him, too! So I slipped outside and hid in the shadows. When I jumped out yodeling...well, there are hardly words to describe my younger brother's reaction! Sparks flew as he barked, jumped, then hit the trail to the house. Yes, I thought it was hilarious. That night, my siblings and I laughed at the success of that escapade—that is, all except the victim. He didn't say much, though he remained white as a sheet. He later admitted that he had just wondered,

What if there is someone around that corner? and when I *did* pop out, it was the last straw for him.

When we listened to a lecture about the influence older siblings have on their younger siblings, the Lord convicted me I should be protecting my younger brother, not teasing him. Though I meant fun, he didn't see it that way. As my parents say, "If it's not fun for everyone, it is *not* fun!" I did not realize how it made him feel until I thought about it this way—I certainly do not like being made fun of by someone older. Younger siblings crave the acceptance of their older siblings; teasing causes them to feel rejection. The jokes you may think are funny may not be viewed as such by your siblings, so be careful!

Encouraging Our Sisters

It has been such a blessing to watch my younger sister mature and grow up in the past few years. The Lord has pointed out to me that I need to seek to be the kind of older sister to her that I would want to have. Because Rachael is several years younger than I, it has been an area I have had to work at to make her a special part of my life. Our younger siblings love to have "big sister" include them; this makes them feel special. I have realized the little things can mean a lot to my sister, such as wearing matching clothes, taking the time to arrange her hair like mine, looking out for her interests, including her in my projects, encouraging her spiritually, or asking for her opinion in areas that she is knowledgeable. Memorizing Scripture together is strengthening as well. Recently, Rachael and I began reading a few verses in the Bible together each night, which has been a blessing. I enjoy our "girly" conversations, and the late-night talks and laughs we have as we drift off to sleep.

Encouraging Manly Brothers

Do you realize what a great influence you have in your brothers' lives? My life is helping mold my brothers into the kind of men they will become. It humbles me to think that the traits my brothers see in me also is chiefly how they will think of womanhood, and also what they someday will look for in a wife.

I deeply regret the opportunities I have allowed to slip past, when I could have positively influenced my brothers' lives. I have lost so much precious time, and I am now learning from my mistakes. I want to encourage you to redeem the days you have with your brothers now; the way you use this time may influence generations. Our lives are impacting the kind of husband, father, and leader they will be as they become men. We have an opportunity today to encourage these future fathers to live in a way which will honor the Lord—we can influence potentially hundreds of descendants. How awing!

We want our brothers to be manly and courageous, ready to face the battles in today's society. I Chronicles 28:20 commands men to *"be strong and of good courage."* Our culture tears down the masculinity of men and discourages them from standing up to their duty. As daughters of the King, we should encourage our brothers to stand firm in their godly role. In their book, Anna Sofia and Elizabeth Botkin write,

> "Our society revels in dragging men down. If we have brothers, we need to remember what they really are is men-in-development, who are having a fierce war waged against them...They will need to be the leaders, initiators, protectors, providers, prophets, priests, and kings to their wives and children. The way we treat our brothers can affect how they perceive masculinity, how they will view their wives, how they will treat their children, and what kind of stand they will take in our culture."[1]

When we simply act like a lady, we encourage our brothers to be strong and manly. Allowing them to open doors and thanking them with a smile encourages them to be gentlemen. Serving them and caring for their well-being encourages them to, in turn, care for and protect us as women. We should encourage their chivalrous acts, but never take their deference for granted. It is an honor to have manly brothers, therefore we should thank them for standing up for and protecting women. We should show even our "little brothers" respect for their role as men.

It is important we support our brothers' goals and show them respect. When we ask their opinion, we show honor and esteem for their leadership. This especially blesses the relationship a sister has with her older brother. They need to be looked up to with respect. In this way, we can encourage them to be responsible and masculine. I try to seek my brothers' opinions, ask their thoughts on things I am writing about, or include them in projects. When appropriate, I also strive to advise them in godly traits. Big sister Rachael MacAlpine (17) shares,

"*I* HAVE FOUR younger brothers, and as their sister, I have a great influence on their development. The reality of my influence is a sobering realization, and it quickens me in living a godly and responsible life—both as a helper to them, and as an example of biblical femininity. I know my conduct and attitudes will not only help form them, but it will also affect their views, attitudes, and their etiquette with women in general. So, how can I best help them become godly men, and gentlemen as well? My oldest brother suggested that respecting them would be the greatest help, adding that respect is a major need for a young man as he matures and takes on more responsibility. True, the Bible instructs women to 'respect their husband' in Ephesians 5:33. For this reason, I purpose to encourage my brothers towards manhood, hoping and believing with them as they learn to lead and to serve, and being available to lend a hand towards their manly exploits. Helping our brothers become young men, helps us become better helpers, too! Everything we do will influence those around us. Let us be prayerful in all things, that our influence would be both prosperous to men and glorious to God."

Our brothers aspire to be like others whom we admire. As they see you respect a certain character trait in someone, they will want to display that as well. They desire your admiration, so encourage godly examples: if you are reading about George Washington, point out godly character qualities he portrayed. When I compliment certain traits in men, my brothers perk up. I may say something like, "When that elderly lady picked up a heavy load, a young man walked across the parking lot to offer to carry it to her car for her," Or, "John carries on a mature conversation with older men and seeks out their company, not his peers." When they hear this, my brothers are encouraged to grow in these areas, and they desire to emulate these things in their own life. In the same way, I should also be vigilant to look for the areas my brothers have grown in, and praise *their* manliness. I have encouraged certain traits in my brothers for many years, and they are now growing in those areas. It has been a slow process—but it is such a blessing to see my brothers grow and mature into men. I encourage you to point out areas of chivalry in your brothers' lives. But remember not to highlight others' good traits to point out your brothers' shortcomings. Remember to notice your brothers' strong points, and compliment in love.

It has been a blessing to read books together with my brothers, or to recommend good books I have read. When we read the same book, we enjoy talking about the story together. Encouraging our brothers to read profitable and worthwhile books is just one way we can encourage their maturity and growth.

Show your brothers they are important to you. In the same way you honor your father when he comes home from work, greet your brothers when they have been away as well. Listen to their latest adventure, offer to help with their school work, and encourage them as they learn new skills. Ask your brother to teach you how to skin the raccoon he just trapped—or whatever interesting project your brother might be working on right now—even if you naturally shrink from the task. This has been an interesting venture for my brother, Nathan, and me!

If you feel your brothers never pay attention to the way you treat them, do not despair. I have found in most cases, when a sibling does not listen to me, it is a result of an unkind way I have previously treated them. Or when a sibling is acting abnormally rowdy, it is usually because they want attention. My natural reaction to this kind of behavior is to ignore or rebuke them. But the Lord has convicted me that a more fruitful and loving remedy is to give them attention—in a nice way— stopping what I am doing, looking them in the eye, and praising them for something well done.

As your brothers see you treating them with respect, they will notice your change. But remember, it really does not matter how your brothers respond. Two wrongs do not make a right. It is still your responsibility to do what the Lord has *you* to do. You must trust the results to God; be patient and persevere. Your efforts will reap rewards in God's time! Ashley, who has two older brothers, testifies of the work the Lord has done in her brother relationships when she had a change of heart,

"*I* CAN CONFIRM that the way one's brothers act is a direct result to how their sister treats them. As a little girl, I was very independent. About that time my mother became ill, and for over a year was nearly bedridden. With a dad gone at work every day and a

CHAPTER FOUR – The Family Sister

mother in bed, I took every opportunity that I could to climb trees and sail away on dreams. As a last resort, my mother had my brothers track and haul me back inside, kicking and screaming. From then on, I never missed a chance to be nasty to them. I always lost in fights, but with my stubbornness, it made me boil. I stored up all that wrath in my heart and became one very unpleasant little sister.

"This unhappy situation went on for many years, with each year bringing me closer to God and that, in turn, helping me to control my stubbornness and independence. One day the Lord brought the golden rule to mind, 'Do unto others as you would have them do unto you,' and I finally understood. I finally viewed myself through my brothers' eyes, and what I saw made me shudder. I realized my job was to simply love, for love worketh no ill.

"I started to greet my brothers each morning. I stopped returning blows, and I bid them good night before going to bed, I learned to bake their favorite cookies and bread, I did small things for them. It was hard at first—my brothers still said things that hurt, and it took many bitten-tongue moments on my part. Yes, I did reply sometimes with a sharp tongue, but it only made the matter worse.

"Slowly my brothers realized that I really had changed, and that I was not going to be mean anymore. My dream came true. I will forever remember the night when one of them went to bed before I did, and bid me good night!

"It took over four years, but my brothers are my best friends now. I now have two 'bodyguards,' as I call them. When we attend a concert I never lack for an arm; when they drive me somewhere they rarely forget to open my door for me. They enjoy cooking with me and singing together, and we often do athletic activities together. My brothers are now my best friends."

Your encouragement will be a great blessing to your brothers as they are striving to grow into manhood. Use your God-given influence in your men's lives for His glory.

The Power of Words

"You are so generous—thank you for helping me!"
"Thank you for your cheerful attitude. You are pleasing God by that!"
"You are very diligent to practice your violin!"

Our words have incredible consequences—in them are the power to bless and uplift, or discourage and destroy. Our siblings are greatly influenced by our words, especially our thoughtful and kind words. The sweetness of fitly spoken words can brighten their entire day! Proverbs 25:11 says, *"A word fitly spoken is like apples of gold in pictures of silver."* Just one word of encouragement can work miracles in my siblings' lives. One smile can brighten their attitude in a second. A simple "Thank you!" can do wonders. Our brothers and sisters need to know we love and appreciate them; make a point to say "I love you" to them, point out tasks they have accomplished well. When you praise them in the presence of your parents, it will especially encourage your siblings.

I think that many older sisters struggle with being bossy—at least I do! I tend to look at my siblings' faults, and I often neglect praising them. Encouragement builds up our family; criticism tears down. *"Every wise woman buildeth her house: but the foolish plucketh it down with her hands"* (Proverbs 14:1). Do I really want to destroy my family? *Am I willing to sacrifice a relationship* with my dear family members just to criticize? I have to tell myself—make a conscious effort—to look for areas to encourage in my siblings' lives, because it is natural for me, when walking past a sibling, to mentally scrutinize them and correct things they are doing. How easy it is for me to set a higher standard for my siblings' actions than I am willing to follow. I am not the one responsible to correct my brothers and sister; that is my parents' job. Truly, what harm is there in some of the things my siblings may be doing? Sure, it might annoy me, but are they really *hurting* anything? Why am I correcting them—because they are sinning against God, or just annoying me? It is usually better if I either remain quiet, or praise something else they are doing well.

One day a sibling said to me, "You have not said one thing nice to me today!" That was sobering. When I fail to praise my siblings, it is a result of pride. This is so selfish; I must overcome my pride to build up others. Have you observed someone wholeheartedly praise another? Praise never hurts the giver. In fact, when I see a sister humbly praise her siblings, I am awed and encouraged. A humble heart is such a beautiful and rare thing to behold. Why am I so afraid to display it?

Something small to me can mean a lot to my siblings—a few words of encouragement can brighten their entire day—a few extra minutes spent to write them a note means more to them than I may imagine! But words can also quickly damage. An especially harsh tone or a few wrong words such as, "What is wrong with you? You've done that two times already today!" can hurt more than we know. *But the tongue can no man tame; it is an unruly evil, full of deadly poison*" (James 3:8). You can probably think back and remember a time when someone from whom you desired approval wounded you with carelessly harsh words. Our siblings yearn for our acceptance and will do much to earn it. Sister, choose your words carefully!

In a sermon by Dr. S. M. Davis,[2] he made a good point: we should praise others—but praise the right thing. We should not praise a talent, but the diligence in developing that talent. A good idea is to make a list of biblical character traits and daily find at least one quality that each sibling has demonstrated and praise them for that particular trait.

Encouragement will certainly inspire growth more than belittlement will. How likely are we to listen to someone who is constantly nagging us about our faults? Would we not listen to and strive to please someone who is always encouraging and helping us, though? "*Pleasant words are as honeycomb, sweet to the soul and health to the* bones" (Proverbs 16:24). In *Making Brothers and Sisters Best Friends*, Sarah Mally says,

> "It has been said that we should praise ten times for every one time we criticize. You will find that you will accomplish much more in the life of your brother or sister if you focus on praising their strengths, rather than pointing out their weaknesses."[3]

It is a struggle to control our tongue, but one word at a time, we can extinguish a habit of criticism. Why don't we start encouraging others and do to them as we would like others to treat us?

Written words of encouragement can also serve as a route of blessing. I have found my siblings love to receive little notes, and when I have given them cards, it is so fruitful; they often write back to me, and then to each other. It is a gift that keeps giving to the entire family! Write a note to your sibling and find a little nook to hide it in—on her pillow, in his school book, under their change of clothes…it is a nice surprise to receive a cute card with a few stickers, knowing big sister appreciates you!

Time is Slipping By

Children grow up and mature so quickly. I feel both eager anticipation to the coming years my siblings and I will enjoy together, and also trepidation as I realize this season together will not last long. Enjoy each day you have with your siblings—treasure their sweet smiles, their cute sayings, their messes, the opportunities you have to serve them. Do not wait to invest in their lives. At times I have found myself thinking, *When we grow up we will have a better relationship than we do now.* Or, *When I am married I will treat my siblings and children better than I do now.* Changing circumstances will not fix a heart-problem; we must allow the Lord to strengthen our relationships *now*!

CHAPTER FOUR — *The Family Sister*

In the big picture, there really are only a few years that we have to help mold our siblings' lives. Think generationally—your siblings will grow up and raise up the next generation. You face the opportunity today to influence countless lives right in the home as your siblings daily grow older. The little things you do and words you say to your siblings today can change the destiny of generations to come. Will you use this precious formative time with your siblings for the furtherance of the glory and Kingdom of God?

on my shelf... RELATED RESOURCES

AUDIO:
- *The Influence of Older Children On Younger Ones* by Dr. S.M. Davis (Solve Family Problems, Lincoln, IL 62656, 800.500.8853; www.solvefamilyproblems.com)

BOOKS:
- *Making Brothers and Sisters Best Friends* by the Mallys (Tomorrow's Forefathers, P.O. Box 11451, Cedar Rapids, IA 52410; www.brothersandsisters.net)
- *Noble Girlhood* by Tiffany Schlichter (Virtuous Daughters, P.O. Box 98, Willis, TX 77378)
- *The Basket of Flowers* by Christoph Von Schmid (reprinted by Lamplighter Publishing, P.O. Box 777, Waverly, PA 18471, 888.246.7635; www.lamplighter.net)
- *Dear Princess* by Mrs. Mary Landis (Rod & Staff Publisher Inc., P.O. Box 3, Highway 172, Crockett, KY 41413, 606.522.4348)

> *"Lo, children are an* **heritage** *of the LORD:*
> *& the fruit of the womb is his reward."*
>
> —PSALM 127:3

family daughters...
REBEKAH & ANNA PARISH

Seeking to carry out God's will for me in sisterhood has prompted a strengthening of conviction in many areas of my life—mostly because I have had to fight my sinful nature at every turn. In the hope that the foothold Satan had in my life can be spared from you my fellow sisters, I am going to share what the Lord, in His grace, has revealed to me.

Let me make an illustration from everyday, practical life. I am busy in the kitchen trying to get bread in the oven for lunch, and at the same time conscious that I have a science test to finish before tomorrow, an email to write, and not to mention finishing a chapter in a really good book. As I barely touch on the list all the things I need (or was it *want?*) to do with my day, I feel a tug on my skirt and look down to hear my little brother saying excitedly, "Oh, Bekah, can I help you make bread? You said I could next time!" My first response to this complication of events would normally be, "Oh dear! I really do not feel like doing this right now, of all times!" On cue as usual, my flesh takes advantage of my inclination to weakness and reasons that letting a five-year-old help me make bread is more work than I should have to deal with. It means more mess, more unnecessary time, and more effort. It means I will have to set what I would like to do aside.

Nevertheless, recently I realized the joy that comes from rejecting my fleshly sentiments, and handling situations such as these in light of God's Word. Scripture commands me to *"In lowliness of mind let each esteem other better than themselves.*

Look not every man on his own things, but every man also on the things of others. Let this mind be in you, which was also in Christ Jesus: Who, being in the form of God, thought it not robbery to be equal with God: But made himself of no reputation, and took upon him the form of a servant" (Philippians 2:3-7). Jesus lowered Himself to a level I cannot comprehend—and His obedience to God and love for me was what brought Him to make the choice. How much more should I, out of gratitude to Him, set aside my own desires and interests to take on "the very nature of a servant" so that my siblings might be able to see that Jesus Christ is Lord through me?

I am convinced that the blessings of sisterhood far outweigh the sacrifices that have to be made—which are really of such little significance! The delighted smile that instantly brightens my little brother's face when I say, "You know what, Isaac, I would really like your help with making bread today: I always enjoy our time together!" is a reward in itself, especially when I consider that I am showing him an example of Christ's selflessness. Words have an impact far greater than I can know. I can use them to either build up or tear down. Scripture says "*The wise in heart shall be called prudent: and the sweetness of the lips increaseth learning*" (Proverbs 16:21). If I am focused on the Lord and asking Him consistently for wisdom, my words and actions will encourage and edify.

William Wilberforce, the abolitionist whose life of sacrifice and servitude turned the tide of the slave industry, once put it this way: "When your heart wants to please God in all things, the very mundane tasks of daily living become acts of worship." All sisters who are really and truly seeking to please God would tell you that the task of investing in siblings is not really a task in the negative sense. It's a responsibility ordained by God to bring joy to both parties—because in working together in fixing our eyes on Jesus, and running the race with perseverance, our daily life quickly becomes an act of sincere and authentic worship, and then the joy accompanies us in whatever work we have to do throughout the day.

—*Rebekah (15)*

"GOD PUTS US in families so we can learn patience—not because we have it already!" a dear friend once told my sister and I with a laugh. This goes for just about every attribute the Word of God encourages us to have: faith, self-control, kindness, humility, and a gentle and quiet spirit. In fact, most of the deepest-impressing lessons I have learned have been revealed to me through serving my siblings. There are moments of trial, as I am always battling my sinful nature, but my siblings bring many moments of joy, too.

In the last year or two, the Lord made me painfully aware that I was using my God-given gifts in the wrong ways. By focusing on my needs, and my desires, I was not serving my family or "administering God's grace." My prayer has become *"Search me, O God, and know my heart: try me, and know my thoughts: and see if there be any wicked way in me, and lead me in the way everlasting"* (Psalms 139:23, 24).

Just recently, after teaching some of my younger sisters and brothers how to knit, I found that doing it together and sharing the joy of a completed project has been so much more fun than doing it alone! They are so excited to make little hats for premature babies at local hospitals, and it also makes them feel special to help those in need. When I include them in my school studies and projects, not only am I keeping them occupied, but I am also building a better relationship with them. The Lord has and still is using my siblings to test my heart; more and more I am realizing the "offensive ways in me." He has been faithful to answer my prayer and is continually showing me that sharing my gift of creativity with my siblings is so much more a joy than keeping it all to myself. I Peter 4:10 teaches that, *"As every man hath received the gift, even so minister the same one to another, as good stewards of the manifold grace of God."* These are perfect times for me to be an example to them by not losing my patience even though someone is knotting up the yarn, has a serious case of the giggles, is making a mess with the glue, or has to go to the bathroom for the third time. It's never easier to include my siblings in what I am doing. They take more time to teach, and make more opportunities for—you guessed it—exemplifying Christ's love and administering God's grace!

I am so thankful that His grace is sufficient. We can say confidently, as Paul did, *"When I am weak, then am I strong,"* and *"I can do all things through Christ which strengtheneth me."*

—Anna (13)

REBEKAH & ANNA PARISH are sisters who seek to be the Lord's hands and feet in whatever way He sees fit. Since it is through God's grace that they have this ministry, their hope and prayer is that they will be able to help turn their siblings' hearts towards an understanding and love for Jesus.

"With my whole heart have I *sought* Thee:
O let me not wander from Thy commandments
Thy word have I *hid* in mine heart,
that I might not sin against Thee.

"With my lips have I *declared*
all the judgments of Thy mouth.
I have *rejoiced* in the way of Thy testimonies,
as much as in all riches.

"I will *meditate* in Thy precepts,
& have *respect* unto Thy ways.
I will *delight* myself in Thy statutes:
I will *not forget* Thy word."

[PSALM 119:10-16]

CHAPTER FIVE

A *Pillar*
OF *S*TRENGTH

*P*ILLARS MUST BE STRONG to support their load. The only source of true strength is our Lord Jesus. He alone will enable us to fulfill the role we carry of blessing our families. When we keep our eyes focused on Him, He will help us live righteously.

Too often, I believe, we try to do good works for the Lord instead of spending the time *with* Him, getting to know *Him* better. We must abide *in* Christ so He can work through our lives. This is the biggest step in leading a life of fruitfulness, for only through Him can we bear fruit. We are nothing outside of our Vine, as John 15:4 puts it: *"As the branch cannot bear fruit of itself, except it abide in the vine; no more can ye, except ye abide in me."* Our relationship with God lays the foundation of our life, and spending time with Him builds this all-important relationship. Making this time a reality in our life is a small sacrifice in comparison with the great reward of close fellowship with the Almighty God!

Christ wants to continue the purification and sanctification work in our lives which He began in our heart at salvation. Ephesians 5:25 says,

"*Christ also loved the church, and gave himself for it; that he might sanctify and cleanse it with the washing of water by the word.*" We must continue to walk in His Spirit and dwell on His Word, so He can make us a spotless sanctuary for His abiding presence.

To abide in Christ, first we must learn Who He is. We must know Jesus' character and discover His will for our lives, and when we study the way He lived His life on earth, we will begin to comprehend these things. I find such strength in Christ's example by thinking of how He responded in everyday situations. Deana Meyers, in her book *I Will Give You The Rain*, shares,

> "Having a better understanding of His humanity prods me to greater obedience. It is all about pleasing my best Friend! Having a better understanding of His humanity causes me to want to do exactly what He did when faced with a trying situation."[1]

Each day Christ faced trials; He was not excluded from the temptations of the flesh. Because He had to resist these temptations, He completely understands our struggles. We should study how He responded in these situations to find guidance for the decisions we face daily. What a comforting fact we discover in Hebrews 4:15—"*For we have not a high priest which cannot be touched with the feeling of our infirmities; but was in all points tempted like as we are, yet without sin.*" He suffered physical hunger, thirst, pain, and spiritual temptations when He did not have to—He could have remained in Heaven's perfectness. This is love that I cannot fathom, but it gives me an intense yearning to know Him better, to fellowship with Him, and commit my life to Him.

We must learn to be guided completely by God, following our Savior's example, Who obeyed His Father to the utmost. We must follow God's leading in daily situations. The Holy Spirit often communicates God's will to us, and we must listen to and obey it! "*Grieve not the Holy Spirit of God, whereby ye are sealed unto the day of redemption*" (Ephesians 4:30). My friend Emily recently shared with me some thoughts on heeding the promptings of the Spirit,

> "I have been asking the Lord to give me a heart that is tender and sensitive to the leading of His Spirit, even in the 'little' things. God is teaching me how important it is to be continually surrendered so that He can make me more like Jesus. I have found this is much easier said than done! At first I may wonder 'Why?', but God has a purpose for everything, and who am I to say this to my Creator? Our Father is so loving, so patient!"

We must heed the Spirit of God, which often works through our conscience. These promptings may come even in the little things—like the night I was heading to bed, exhausted from a long day. As I passed the dryer, somehow I sensed that there might be a load of clothes that I had not folded earlier that afternoon. Hoping I could just ignore this suspicion, I continued on my way to bed. The Spirit immediately pricked, *Whatsoever ye do, do it heartily, as to the Lord,* but I pushed the uneasy naggings out of my mind. *I'm tired, and it can wait. I've already folded three loads today.* The words of my parents then come to mind, *Did you do everything to the best of your ability?* Still determinedly headed to bed, the Spirit would not give up on me! *Grieve not the Holy Spirit of God!* Before I could counter with any other argument, I turned around and headed back to that dryer—which as I suspected, was full. The promptings of the Spirit are a blessing, which prods us in the narrow way of the Lord. We must not resist it! *"Quench not the Spirit"* (I Thessalonians 5:19). We are to obey His will, and ask for His power to do so.

Prayerfully Abiding

We cannot produce any truly good work through our own strength,[2] and as we live in the holy presence of Jesus, the Father is glorified through our lives.[3] Thus, we should not limit our fellowship with God to a set amount of time. Instead, we should work up to a tithe of our waking hours—of meditating and abiding constantly in Him.

> "Abide in me, and I in you. As the branch cannot bear fruit of itself, except it abide in the vine; no more can you, except you abide in me. I am the vine, you are the branches: He that stays in me, and I in him, the same brings forth much fruit: for without me you can do nothing... Herein is my Father glorified." (John 15:4,5,8)

We must be vigilant in focusing on our Savior throughout the day. Prayer and communication with Christ are an important key to abiding in Him. We should constantly come to our Lord in prayer throughout the day—and night. Strive to talk with Jesus constantly: as you work outside or listen to your siblings' chatter or wash the dinner dishes—whatever the situation, turn to Him in prayer. Delight in dwelling on His love. Make Him your most cherished thought, your closest Friend.

While we must be in prayer incessantly, it is good to specifically set aside time each day to pray in a quiet place. When I kneel down and pray in the name of Jesus my Intercessor, it helps me feel as though I were sitting at His feet. I feel such a need of God's grace, and a closeness to Him who freely gives it. For years, I never knelt down to pray; honestly, I was embarrassed of showing my need before man. Once I did kneel to pray, it helped me to pour out my heart as I acknowledged my humble state in the presence of a holy and sovereign God. *"O come, let us worship and bow down: let us kneel before the* LORD *our maker"* (Psalm 95:6). What a blessed thing to kneel at the feet of Jesus!

Dwelling in the Spirit

> "But the fruit of the Spirit is love, joy, peace, long-suffering, gentleness, goodness, faith, meekness, temperance... They that are Christ's have crucified the flesh with the affections and lusts. If we live in the Spirit, let us also walk in the Spirit." (Galatians 5:22-25)

CHAPTER FIVE — *A Pillar of Strength*

Our minds must be kept pure, and our thoughts regulated by the will of Christ. We need to evaluate every area of life and every thing we put into our mind—is it virtuous, lovely, pure, and praiseworthy, according to Philippians 4:8? What you "feed" your mind has a great impact on where your thoughts will be, so ask yourself, "Are the books I read profitable—do they encourage me to grow in Christ?" "Are my friends examples of godliness?" "Is the music I listen to God-glorifying?" "Would I show this to Jesus if He were staying in our home?" or "Would Jesus read this?" Since our body *is* the temple of the Lord, we must "feed" and care for it as we would Christ Himself, according to I Corinthians 6:19.

I have found that my thoughts set the tone for my day and have a large impact on whether I dwell in Christ or not through the hours—and even when I think my mind is occupied by a task at hand, there seems to always be a larger thought in the back of my mind. One thing that helps me to start my day right, centered on Christ, is to focus my first thought every morning on Him—before I even open my eyes. I am constantly trying to put this into practice, and it has helped me tremendously in keeping my mind stayed on Him throughout the rest of the day. My mom has read that it only takes a few weeks to form a habit, so I want to develop a habit of turning my thoughts over to the Lord each morning.

In a similar way, what I think about before I go to sleep affects my night "thoughts" and what I wake up thinking the next day. Sometimes before I go to sleep we listen to hymns. During the night if I wake up, I am amazed to find I am still humming that last stanza in my mind. Or, as I go to sleep if I am trying to figure out a problem I am having with web design, all night I dream about it—what is amazing, is that sometimes during my sleep I figure out the problem! So, I recently realized that I need to make a point to go to sleep thinking about Jesus. If the last thing I read at night is a verse or two from the Bible, which is kept easily accessible by my bedside, I wash my mind with God's Word and direct my thoughts to Him throughout the night. During the night if I awaken, I also strive to go to God in prayer and meditation of memorized Scripture, as did King David.[4] The night hours are a perfect time to pray, because the cares and responsibilities of life are dimmed.

Daily Time with Christ

It is also important we schedule a time each day to spend reading God's Word, in a quiet atmosphere. As we establish this as a regular habit in our life at the same time each day, our hearts will be more prepared. Like any other relationship, the more time we spend with Him, the more we will look forward to and treasure it.

My journey of daily devotions with my Creator has only begun, and has been an incredible blessing in my spiritual walk. Soon after I turned thirteen, I made morning devotions a regular part of my life. When I began diligently searching God's Word and spending time with Him, the Lord began working greatly in my heart. This has proved to be a spiritual investment that I would never trade; it has been truly worth the effort to diligently read the Bible each morning. I urge you to make this a daily habit in your life if you have not already done so, especially while you are young. You will always be thankful you made this commitment. Karissa shares her testimony of developing a daily quiet time:

> "*I* REMEMBER SEVERAL years ago, talking to some dear sisters in the Lord about my quiet time. I had not established one and it seemed like I could not attain victory in this area. Some excerpts from journal entries within the last few years read:
>
> *"A friend asked how my prayer life is. Terrible! I told her all year I've probably spent two hours in prayer, rather than the many I could have: one hour a day, would be over 300 hours a year. She told me these are very serious matters. She encouraged me to wake up early and spend an hour with Him each day.'*

CHAPTER FIVE — *A Pillar of Strength*

"'Dad asked us to spend five minutes of quiet reflection in the Word this morning. That time was incredible. If five minutes could be so strengthening, where could my spiritual life be a year from now if I spent an hour every morning with Him, walked in His presence, and fellowship moment by moment?'

"By the Lord's grace, I was able to establish a regular morning quiet time. When I have sought the Lord in my daily quiet time, delighting in spending time with Him as my dearest Friend, there have been incomparable blessings.

"If you have not established a daily quiet time with the Lord—whether morning, afternoon, or evening—I encourage you to do so. Allow His still, small voice to speak to your heart. Ask the Lord to apply to your life what you have learned. Wait on Him; be still and know that He is God (Psalm 46:10). Do not allow your time with the Lord to become a task or drudgery, but be sure your communion with Him is open by a cleansed, unfeigned heart, and keep a sweet relationship of delight with Him. The only things of eternal value are our relationship with the Lord and our investment for His Kingdom. You can never regret this commitment. I have certainly not claimed perfection in this area of the quiet time. There have been ups and downs, times where I have had to refocus, reprioritize, when I have realized my quiet time was beginning to slip. And through those times of struggle I have realized how many blessings are missed when one does not faithfully meet with the Lord in meaningful Bible reading/study and true prayer.

"The riches of grace and the closeness to our dear Savior are so worth the sacrifice of establishing a quiet time. You will soon find that this time is not a sacrifice at all, but a true delight and joy. It will become the highlight of your day, and you may find yourself fleeing to His Word throughout the day for more of His grace, more of Him!"[5]

The purpose of a devotion time with the Lord is to listen to His voice, open our heart to Him in prayer, read His word, and enjoy His holy presence away from the distractions of the world. Spend this time with your Savior as you would a good friend—because this is really building the foundation with your closest Friend. As you deepen this relationship and discover the joys of His presence, you will cherish this time with your Savior more and more. You will look forward to reading His Word. It is similar to our physical appetites; we develop a desire for what we feed our minds—a few years ago, my mom began cooking healthier foods for us, incorporating fresh and nutritious foods into our diet. At first, I did not find satisfaction in those foods—I wanted *white* bread, not seven-grain wheat bread! As my Mom would eat a salad with more nuts, vegetables, and unidentifiable critters on it than I could count, she would say, "One day you will desire a nutritious diet—you just have to get used to it!" I half-way believed her, yet after many months of eating a more healthy diet, I did find these foods satisfying and soon I *loved* salads. The day came when the thought of fried chicken made my stomach hurt, and chocolate gave me a headache! Today, I crave natural, pure foods which God has blessed us with—though I admit that I still do not have an appetite for the very colorful salads which my mom eats. Similarly, the more you read the Bible and discover its rich "nutrients," anything less than His Word will become dry in comparison. I encourage you to weed out areas of your life—whether it be certain books, media, music, or friends—that distract you from the richness of God's Word.

Distractions need to be minimized during the time we spend with the Lord. Books, the phone ringing, or a list of things to do—these things distract me during my devotions when they are in sight. They need to be removed so I can concentrate on the Word. Before you begin your time with the Lord, try to eliminate distractions and focus your mind solely on Jesus. When we are fully listening and open to His instruction, we will be able to hear His words to us. A friend shares,

"A good way to start your devotions is by getting rid of all distractions. Find that spot in your house or outside where you can be alone. Ask God to open the eyes of your heart as you read His Word. Just like Samuel say, '*Speak; for thy servant heareth*' (1 Samuel 3:10). Then truly listen! Sometimes when I open my Bible, and there is just the verse I need to read. Other times when I am reading a certain book in the Bible, if I am truly listening, God will point out what I need to work on or meditate on for that day."

I find if I have my devotions first thing in the morning, it prepares me for the day ahead, so I have mine right after I get up every day. "*My voice shalt thou hear in the morning, O Lord; in the morning will I direct my prayer unto thee*" (Psalm 5:3). Normally I read at least a chapter in the Bible each day, but sometimes if I do not have as much time to spend as normal, I read just a few verses. I read through books of the Bible, though occasionally I'll skip around, going through different passages as the Lord leads and as I am learning about related subjects. For example, last year I read about Paul's evangelistic journeys, so I decided to read about his missionary travels in Acts. This year I took a college course on the Old Testament, so I read the Prophetic books during that time and gained much insight.

You can also follow a reading schedule, often found in devotional books. Another idea is to keep a "spiritual gem" journal as you read—when you come across a verse that the Lord speaks to you through, jot it down with some notes. You can also write down a verse for the day to dwell on. I have found Bible searches on certain topics to be very interesting and profitable. Once I did a search through Psalms for ways to praise God, and wrote down these gems as I came across them. More recently, I searched for every reference of Jesus in the book of Romans, because I wanted to learn more about Christ's character in order to apply these lessons to my everyday life. Through these references, I found how His love and obedience was repeatedly referred to and how He obeyed the Father. He was obedient unto death, obedient enough to go to the cross. Romans 5:19 wonderfully points this out: *"For as by one man's disobedience many were made sinners, so by the obedience of one shall many be made righteous."* If Jesus set such an example, should not I also completely obey my Lord and my parents?

One of our dear older friends shared with me the "schedule" she follows during her daily time with the Lord. She loves spending time with God and searching for His "jewels" for hours each morning.

— Begin with prayer. Read until a passage speaks to you. Stop there for the daily reading.
— Copy the verse into your journal.
— Think on the wonderful truth of that verse, and write your thoughts. I like to focus in on 'my part' and 'God's part.' This helps me acknowledge His magnificent promises. It also helps me to clarify in my mind my own responsibilities.
— Ask yourself, 'How does this apply to my life today?' Since He is faithful to meet all our needs, there will always be application.
— I write a brief prayer of thanks for the things I have learned, which is a form of worship. I also enter specific prayer concerns for myself and others.

As well as reading God's Word, we also should pray during our time with Him. We must ask for wisdom to understand His Word. I have been challenged to pray for a solid hour, and though I have not reached this goal, I have found that pouring out my heart to my loving Savior is so refreshing and brings me all the closer to His feet. In *Stepping Heavenward*, Elizabeth Prentiss puts it this way,

> "I sometimes find it a help, when dull and cramped in my devotions, to say to myself: 'Suppose Christ should now appear before you, and you could see Him as He appeared to His disciples on earth, what would you say to Him?' This brings Him near, and I say what I would say if He were visibly present."[6]

CHAPTER FIVE — *A Pillar of Strength*

An Incredible Adventure

Joy had made a commitment at a young age to read the Word each morning. During most devotion times, she felt a wonderful closeness to her Savior, and would be so refreshed by this fellowship with Him. By looking to Christ, her day would go smoothly—aye, she faced trials—but she was abiding in Christ, so she reflected Him in her reactions. But other days, her devotions just seemed...well, stale. Nothing jumped out as she read, and she could not seem to concentrate as she tried to pour out her heart to Christ. The Word seemed so far away, and her actions felt like a ritual—just something else to check off the list. Joy would read a chapter in the Word, mumble a prayer which resembled, "Lord, help me to do better today than yesterday!" Then off she would go, "trying to live a good life for the Lord." But as she rushed off, who would meet her but little brother who had just caught a prized frog. He would proudly display, "Look what I found!" Irritated, Joy would push him away, wondering why he had to get in her way this morning, of all days, just when she had resolved to do better. The day wears on in similar fashion, yet she never stops to look to Him who reaches out with those nail-pierced hands to help. At the end of the day Joy would fall into bed exhausted and discouraged, wondering why she hadn't succeeded in her attempts to be more Christ-like. She would tell herself, *I will just have to try harder tomorrow!* Days may roll by in similar fashion. Finally, she reaches her rope's end, not able to

> "*I find that it is* not only hard to get away and spend time with Jesus, but it also sometimes feels like I am not getting anything out of it—I read, yet nothing 'jumps' out. Is it then unprofitable? No, because it does help even if we can not feel it. It is like taking potatoes and holding them under running water. Even though a lot of dirt may not come off, they still are cleansed to a degree. So I should just continue reading. It will cleanse my heart and make it good soil for growing fruit."
>
> —Sharia Buckingham at age 21

do anything but fall limp with empty hands at the feet of her Lord. Joy cries out to Him, sobbing for help. She lays there in the darkness, realizing she has nothing to bring Him, and wonders, *What was the problem?* She finally stops to listen to His voice and realizes that *she* has been the problem. He was there all along the way, but she had lost focus of Him. How Jesus rejoices when she finally gives up and cries to Him for strength. He simply wanted her to come to Him because *through* her surrendered life He could do big things. He reminds Joy of the comforting promise found in II Corinthians 12:9—*"My grace is sufficient for thee: for my strength is made perfect in weakness."*

I am ashamed to admit this example is often the story of myself, carrying all too many of my own struggles, instead of bringing them to Christ and focusing on Him. How often I grope along trying to live my days *for* Him, without Him. I too easily fall into the mindset that I am going to do something *for* God. As if anything *I* do is worth anything to Him? What foolishness, that of a child. Jesus did not go the cross because He *needed* me; He died there for me because He *loved* me. The only works that please Him are those that *He* does through me. He wants me to give myself to Him, so He can do a good work in my life—and what He does through me will truly be glorious because it is His doing. *"Whatsoever God doeth, it shall be forever"* (Ecclesiastes 3:14).

When I begin to feel that my devotions are just another "chore" to check off, I must renew my commitment to seek Him. To think the Almighty God would desire to teach me through His Word is so amazing—because this is true, I must use my quiet time wisely. As I read the Words of God, I need to soak them in. I must quiet my heart before His presence. How can I hear His quiet voice if I am rushing through the verses, thinking about what is next on my to-do list for the day?

When I receive a letter from a dear friend, I rarely just toss it on my desk among stacks of other papers to read later, nor do I carelessly glance over what is written. So why should I ever consider doing something like this with the Letters *God* has written for His children? Every portion of the Bible has meaning; every inspired word is a precious revelation from God. Lately, I have been reading in the Old Testament about the tabernacle specifications, priests' clothing and sacrificial requirements for the Israelites. At times, it is easy to think, *What does this mean to me? We're not going to build a tabernacle or sacrifice lambs!* But even in these passages so much can be learned about our God's character—in these laws we find He is a God of detail, order and purity.

As we study the Scriptures, let us notice each word. Study for example, James 1:1: *"James, a servant of God and of the Lord Jesus Christ, to the twelve tribes which are scattered abroad, greeting."* From a glance, this may have seemed to have little meaning for my life; yet—if I look a little further, what a treasure of instruction it contains. If James, Jesus' own earthly brother, considered himself a servant of Christ, how much more am I His servant? I should earnestly pour my life into His work. This is not even studying the entire verse; looking it up in a Bible commentary, we will find much more to be gleaned. God's word is full of "hidden" gems we need to excavate!

Accountability

Be committed in having your daily devotions with God; it will not happen unless you *choose* to do it. Since it is such a defensive sword of protection from temptation, Satan wants to persuade us to go without reading God's Word—and often this comes in subtle ways such as "I don't have enough time to read today!" Even if you do not have time to read much, read and meditate on a few verses. It is better to read a short portion and heed it than hurrying over three chapters anyway! The days when your schedule is especially busy, you will need His strength, wisdom and guidance. *Do not skip* your reading.

A few years ago, my mom started a wonderful idea which has kept me accountable in my daily Bible reading, when she began writing a Bible verse on an index card along with some thoughts each day for me. I have also done the same thing for her every day, sharing an insight from my Bible reading. This is a wonderful way to be accountable to reading the Bible daily. God's Word is a lasting foundation to build a relationship on.

The Sword of the Lord

We must be girded with the armor of God so we can flee sin. When we have inscribed God's perfect Word on our heart, He will also be able to bring it to our mind for encouragement during trials and temptations. One friend, who has memorized several books of the Bible, shares,

> "It really isn't hard to memorize the Bible, whether it is a verse, chapter, or book... We have many chances to memorize God's Word that we don't even think of—during devotions, while washing the dishes, cleaning the house, hanging laundry, getting ready for or laying in bed, or reading it to your younger brother. It is such a wonderful blessing and you never know when you might need it."

For many years, though I knew the importance of Scripture memorization and witnessed several friends memorize, I did not personally made the commitment to do it myself. Finally, the Lord convicted my heart of this need in my life, and I made myself accountable to a godly friend to hide God's Word in my heart. We made a goal to memorize a certain number of verses per week, and since I knew I must tell her at the end of this period of time if I completed the "assignment," it kept me accountable and diligent. These verses have been such a blessing to have on my mind throughout the day, and have helped me abide in Christ. When we hide God's word in our hearts, He will use it to keep our mind stayed on Christ. *"Thy word have I hid in mine heart, that I might not sin against thee"* (Psalm 119:11).

CHAPTER FIVE -- *A Pillar of Strength*

I have found the best way for me to memorize Scripture is to study only a few verses at a time until I have them completely memorized. It is also helpful for me to see the verses throughout the day, so I post verses on cards throughout our home, areas such as my desk, room, or mirror. The entire family can read them as well, when I put them in visible places. I try to recite the verses I am working on throughout the day. I have also found hearing the passages read out loud is helpful, so I listen to recordings of the memory passages.[7]

Singing Bible verses is another method I use in memorizing Scripture—often I sing Psalms put to music.[8] Another option is to put a portion of Scripture to a tune, which works well for those who are musically inclined.

I encourage you to hide the Lord's Word in your heart, using whatever method that best suits you.[9] You will be amazed at the rich blessings that will be cultivated from this investment. The effort you pour into this will be doubly rewarded, as you will never lose these precious truths that will be ingrained in your heart forever. Make yourself accountable to a family member or mature friend and begin with a small goal—two or three verses a week. It is possible, and *truly* worth it! I have witnessed a young friend memorize many books of the Bible; her commitment has been a great inspiration. She has invested hours each day to commit these chapters to heart. I know she will be blessed the rest of her life by those verses. May we make the choice to hide God's precious word deep in our souls.

Another thing that helps me abide in Jesus is to sing hymns. While I am folding clothes or washing dishes or milking the cow, instead of letting my thoughts wander, it is a wonderful opportunity to praise my Lord. It is very helpful to memorize hymns so we can be ready to sing at any time. I thought I knew our favorite hymns by heart, but found out otherwise one day as we were butchering our chickens at our friends' processing plant. As usual, we had engaged in interesting conversation as we dissected chickens at the eviscerating table; after several hours, we had explored every topic from college degrees to electric fence chargers. I asked my friend Rosanna, the owner's daughter, if she wanted to sing hymns while we worked. She agreed, and after deciding on a hymn we both liked, I quickly realized that I did not know all the verses of this familiar hymn! It was embarrassing to find out how unprepared I was to sing without a hymnal. This encouraged me to memorize hymns as I sing, rather than thoughtlessly repeating the words.

Renewing the Focus

The Lord revealed to me recently the need to slow down and rest in Him. I realized I had allowed the busyness of life to crowd Christ from my mind. I penned my thoughts with a sigh in my journal,

> "Life has been busy lately. Today the Lord spoke to me about being too busy. What is my focus? To be honest, I have thought little of Christ during these past weeks—instead I have focused ardently on the current projects I 'need' to do. I stopped to realize, when I am 60 or 70 years old and the world holds no attraction to me, I will look back and think of what a futile youth I led—so multi-focused rather than singly focused on Christ, so bent with my own desires and not willing for His will *alone* to be done, despite the costs."

In *Stepping Heavenward*, one of my favorite inspirational books, these feelings were voiced perfectly.

> "It is high time to stop and think. I have been like one running a race and am stopping to take breath... I feel restless and ill at ease. I see that if I would be happy in God, I must give Him all. And there is a wicked reluctance to do that. I want Him—but I want to have my own way, too. I want to walk humbly and softly before Him and I want to be admired and applauded. To whom shall I yield?"[10]

CHAPTER FIVE — *A Pillar of Strength*

The Lord showed me the importance of refocusing on Him, of putting Him first in my priorities—not allowing other things to put Christ "on the back burner" in my mind. I want to share with you two ways I did this. The first step of this process was to sacrifice *all* of my goals and desires to Him. I read a testimony of an older girl who said she wrote down all of her dreams and desires, and one by one completely surrendered them to the Lord in return for *His* will. Later, she looked back, and realized God had actually fulfilled those dreams in much better ways than she had ever imagined! As I wrote down my desires and dreams and laid them at my Lord's feet, I realized what insignificant sacrifices they were in return for God's greater plan. I stopped trying to do these projects alone, on my own power. I placed them in *His* hands, so that if it was His will for them to be completed, He could work that out. Again, I was reminded that nothing really is "mine," and everything I ever hope to do is because *the Lord* has done it through me.

The second key I found in rejuvenating my spiritual walk was to go on a "diet" of certain things or activities that had been filling my mind. I realized my thoughts had been constantly overwhelmed with cares and things of the world rather than abiding in the peaceful calm of my Savior. Coincidentally, these things which I knew I needed to spend less time doing, were also the hardest things to give up. While they were good projects in themselves, I had allowed them to distract my focus from Christ. So I set aside a specified amount of time to completely stay away from these things, just to invest in my walk with God.

When I "stopped" and fully placed my thoughts on the Lord throughout the day, I felt I had jumped off the fast-paced train of life and reentered the quiet, steady peace of God! My mind felt light; as I went about my regular chores, instead of thinking about something I needed to do, the Lord was able to bring to my mind people who needed prayer. I began to look around once again for chores I could help my family with even though I had not been asked. I no longer felt like I was pushed to go on to the "next thing on the list."

Our focus on Christ can so easily be drawn away by the goals of the world, or envying someone else's life, or things we are "doing for the Lord." We can allow "good" projects to draw us away from a focus on Him and our family. Even if we are still spending time with them, our minds may be elsewhere. What is filling *your* mind today? Projects, friends, news, e-mails, schoolwork? Let us seek to give Christ the throne of our mind and take every thought captive for His glory.

Our Deepest Desire

Sometimes we may feel farther away from Christ, and find it harder to abide in Him. I have learned that when this happens, it is because I have allowed something to come between us. He has not any farther away, but I have lost focus on Him. It is a matter of where my heart truly is—where my primary goal is focused.

In our innermost being, what is our deepest desire? What do we dream to be? Who do we seek to be admired or accepted by? Who do we copy? Where are our thoughts the majority of the time? What are our ambitions? What do we do in our free time? What is our *deepest desire*? By asking ourselves these things, we will find where our heart truly is. When I evaluate my heart in this light, I sheepishly realize how short I fall from allowing my Master to completely guide me. Do I truly give Him Lordship over every moment of my day? Or do I claim areas of my life and choices for myself, not being guided by His will? I need to seek Him with my entire being. I need to seek to imitate *His* likeness, not that of some other person. I must seek to become the woman *He* wants me to be, not to be esteemed by others. My "dreams" need to be what the Lord wants me to do, not personal worldly ambition. I need to reach out of my own self and fill the needs of others, living for His glory.

CHAPTER FIVE — *A Pillar of Strength*

Recording Ebenezers

The story of the Israelites has always intrigued me. God delivering His people from the Egyptians at the last minute, providing water from a rock, sending angel's food from Heaven... the miracles are innumerable. What blessed people to be chosen by God and provided for by His hand. If any had reason to be grateful, the children of Jacob did.

Repeatedly we see a pattern, though—a wonderful miracle is performed on the Israelites' behalf and their lives are spared. They praise God. The next morning, they wake up and realize they are lacking something else; instead of remembering how greatly God worked previously on their behalf, they gripe and complain.[11] What a heart-breaking story of the ungratefulness and unfaithfulness of God's people!

Wait. How many times do I see my own actions and attitudes mirrored in these people? How often have I seen my heavenly Father's abundant goodness poured out on our behalf? God's loving hand is always protecting, guiding, and providing, even when I am unaware. One day I praise God for a providential miracle. The next day I look around and see something else I want. I so quickly forget His mighty deeds.

But God has a remedy; He knows that we humans have forgetful minds. I Samuel 7:12 explains His solution for those with no memory:

> "Then Samuel took a stone, and set it between Mizpeh and Shen, and called the name of it Ebenezer, saying, Hitherto hath the LORD helped us."

Come Thou Fount

Here I raise mine Ebenezer—
Hither by Thy help I'm come;
And I hope by Thy good pleasure
Safely to arrive at Home.

Jesus sought me when a stranger
Wandering from the fold of God;
He to rescue me from danger
Interposed His precious blood.

—Robert Robinson (1735-1790)

Ebenezer means "the stone of help." Samuel erected this stone as a memorial of the victory God had worked on their behalf. This would be a reminder to their children if they were to forget the "impressions of this providence"[12] and it would revive their memories.

It is *vital* we remember all our Almighty God has done! We must erect "ebenezers" of God's wonderful workings; a journal, scrapbook, plaque—anything that will remind us of His works. Begin a special journal and record all the "little" things that the Lord does in your life day by day, as well as the blessings that are overwhelmingly amazing. Our Father is looking for children to praise Him: *"The true worshipers shall worship the Father in spirit and in truth: for the Father seeketh such to worship him"* (John 4:23). We should make it a point to thank God for His hand in our lives—to do more than request, but to be grateful. Let us remember all His mighty deeds. He is worthy to be praised!

The Blessing

God gives a beautiful promise to our faithfulness in *"drawing nigh unto Him"* (James 4:8): He will draw us ever closer to His bosom and we will reap the joys of dwelling in Him. The Lord promises in II Chronicles 7:14, *"If My people who are called by My name will...pray and seek My face...then I will hear from heaven, and will forgive their sin and heal their land."* We, as Christians, need to humble ourselves and seek God's face. This is the starting point of the transformation of an entire nation—when God's people do the right thing, when they seek His face in humiliation—He can use us to change the world around us.

May the Lord abundantly bless and multiply the time you spend with Him. May you stand strong against all the wiles of the Devil,[13] because your mind, spirit, and heart are firmly planted in Jesus Christ.

CHAPTER FIVE – *A Pillar of Strength*

on my shelf... RELATED RESOURCES

-- *Kept For the Master's Use* by Francis Havergal (Keepers of the Faith, P.O. Box 100, Ironwood, MI 49938; *www.keepersofthefaith.com*)

-- *The Saving Life of Christ* by W. Ian Thomas (Zondervan, Grand Rapids, MI 49530)

-- *Each New Day* by Corrie ten Boom (Spire Books, Old Tappan, NJ)

-- *Joel: A Boy of Galilee* by Annie Fellows Johnston (Lamplighter Publishing, P.O. Box 777, Waverly, PA 18471, 888.246.7735; *www.lamplighter.net*)

More Ideas FOR QUIET TIME

Making time for prayer and Bible study is a battle for most people, although without it, we are weak and prone to sin. Spending time with God gives us strength and power. For best results, do not eat anything at least an hour before bed time. You will sleep more peacefully if your body is not digesting food when it needs to rest. Getting sufficient rest is important to a meaningful devotional time. You will feel much more alert the next morning.

-- Start your day with God. By evening you may be too tired to focus on the Bible and prayer.

-- Make it an habit to ask the Lord to open your understanding as you open your Bible.

-- Have a notebook and take notes as God speaks to your heart.

-- Purchase a stack of index cards, and as you find a Bible verse that grips your heart, write it down. Keep it with you and read it throughout the day.

-- As you pray for others, remember to pray for yourself daily to be a good example and witness for Christ.[14] —MRS. CONNIE LINDSEY

a family daughter...
SAMANTHA P.

"*A*S THE HART *panteth after the water brooks, so panteth my soul after thee, O God. My soul thirsteth for...the living God*" (Psalm 42:1-2). This reminds us how we should long to be with our Savior as the deer longs for flowing streams! It is easy to unconsciously long to be conformed to this world, instead of longing to be "*transformed by the renewing of your mind*" (Romans 12:2). It is extremely important to daily spend time with the Lord, so we may resist attacks from the Devil.

Our Lord delights in each moment we set aside to talk to Him. Christ deserves all, not just some, of our praise, adoration, and worship. He should be in our thoughts all the time. Let us act like He lives in us! As I go through my day, I try to consciously think about Christ, meditate on His Word, and talk to Him—tell Him my joys and sorrows. Spending time with our Savior is a privilege, not a burden.

Prayer is one of the best ways we can draw closer to the Lord; it is communicating with God from the heart. In order to understand how we should pray, all we need to do is look to our Savior's prayer as He talked to His Father in Matthew, chapter six. Prayer is so powerful! The Devil knows how powerful prayer is, that is why he is always trying to distract us when we pray. We must "be sober, be vigilant," while we are talking to our Savior, "*your adversary the devil, as a roaring lion, walketh about, seeking whom he may devour: Whom resist steadfast in the faith*" (I Peter 5:8-9).

I enjoy memorizing the Bible, God's love letter. While memorizing Psalm 119, I have been amazed at the depth of the Psalmist's desire to have an intimate relationship with the Lord. It convicted me and made me ask, "How much do I really delight in God's commandments?" The Psalmist loved God's law with all his heart—why should we be different? "O how love I thy law! it is my meditation all the day" (vs. 97). It does not matter what length you memorize—all of it will benefit you for the rest of your life!

Often, God sends trials our way to test and refine us as silver is refined (Psalm 66:10). For the past three years, God has tested my faith more than I could ever have imagined. Through it all He has been faithful; I would never trade these years for anything else. They have brought me closer to the Lord and made me totally depend on Him—not resting in my own strength, because I am nothing apart from Him. It is extremely important that we cultivate a strong relationship with Christ, not only for our own benefit, but that we may better serve Him, our families, and one day, Lord willing, our future husband. May we be like corner pillars cut for the structure of a palace, as we draw closer to our Savior and grow in our walk with the Lord.

SAMANTHA, *age 17, lives with her family in Virginia. She is the oldest of seven children, one whom is with the Lord. She enjoys reading and memorizing God's Word, helping her parents in any way she can, investing in and spending time with her siblings, cooking her family's meals, playing the piano, sewing, & writing letters. She loves the Lord with all her heart and seeks to glorify Him in all she does. She is preparing to be a wife and mother someday if it is the Lord's will. May God be glorified in her life!*

"You can will to choose for your *associates* those who are most devout and holy.

"You can will to read *books* that will stimulate you in your Christian life rather than those that merely amuse.

"You can will to use every means of *grace* appointed by God.

"You can will to spend much time in *prayer* without regard to your frame at the moment.

"You can will to prefer a religion of *principle* to one of mere feeling; in other words, to obey the will of God when no comfortable glow of emotion accompanies your obedience."[1]

[ELIZABETH PRENTISS]

"To be in Christ—that is *redemption*; But for Christ to be in you— that is *sanctification*."[2]

[W. IAN THOMAS]

CHAPTER SIX

A *Humble*
Maidservant

"HELP! I'm stuck!" The sticky silt swallowed my legs as I helplessly sank deeper. I, the one who is always careful to stay clear of any mud, was now covered in filth—not to mention my hopelessly ruined dress. My family, trying to suppress their laughter, stood at a distance with my camera—one of the few times they have voluntarily taken pictures. I floundered, trying to pull myself out of the muck—to no avail. I could not get out of this mess...I was helpless.

A few years ago, we had a pond dam repaired on our property. Since the pond was silted in, the excavation company had to clear it out and make a pile of the muck nearby. When we checked the progress, my younger siblings, always curious and ready for adventure, decided to climb on the pile. They had fun walking on top of it, trying to move fast enough so they would not sink in the stinky sponge-like mud. Being the family photographer, I wanted to get a picture of the opposite side of the pile, so my brother Samuel offered to lead me across. I followed, not realizing just how gooey it was underneath the thin top crust. I also did not consider the difference in our weights; a seven- and sixteen-year-old are quite different in this respect, no matter how big Samuel claims he is! Thus, about five steps later—and one third of the way across the pile—I found myself succumbing quickly into the reeking muck. Soon I was embarrassingly knee-deep, calling for someone to catch my camera. At the cost of my socks, shoes, legs, and arms, I was able to toss it to my amused onlookers. My situation was not very humorous in my eyes, and I had no clue how I was supposed to get out. Let's just suffice to say I did manage to crawl out—eventually. The Lord certainly used this situation to teach me some valuable lessons.

I love comfort and convenience. I dislike being dirty, and I can't stand being helpless. Just as I was unable to help myself out of that physical mess, I am spiritually helpless and filthy in God's eyes. My sins are an odious stench in God's nostrils. *"But we are all as an unclean thing, and all our righteousness are as filthy rags"* (Isaiah 64:6). I am nothing, but my Savior is everything, and He died on the cross to save my soul. He suffered excruciating pain to ransom me from my filthy state.

In II Samuel 7:18, I find a question that I should often ask myself: *"Who am I, O Lord GOD? and what is my house, that thou hast brought me hitherto?"* I am no one without God's grace and salvation; I am nothing without His enabling power in my life; I am capable of nothing without His help; I am condemned to hell without His mercy. I am not my own—I am *"bought with a price"* (I Corinthians 7:23), the blood of Christ. The key to humility is realizing we have nothing of ourselves to glory in, except in *His* cross. This does not mean we are worthless, because we are created in the image of God, but we do need to realize that without God, we are not able to do anything good. *"They are all together become filthy: there is none that doeth good"* (Psalm 14:3).

We are here to glorify God with the life He has given us. Jesus Christ set a pattern for us to follow; His mission was bringing God glory, so

He lived according to His Father's desires. During Christ's short life on earth, He humbly served others—from small children (Matthew 18) to great rulers (Matthew 8:10). Although He was the ruler of the universe, He humbled himself to serve *us*, because it was His Father's will. He challenges, "Who are My servants to do otherwise?"

"If I then, your Lord and Master, have washed your feet; ye also ought to wash one another's feet...The servant is not greater than his lord; neither he that is sent greater than he that sent him. If ye know these things, happy are ye if ye do them." (John 13:14-17)

We are to follow our Lord's example, but because this goes against our naturally selfish and proud nature, we often find it difficult to serve others. We must let Christ's self*less* love overcome our own selfishness. Our selfish nature must wane; our cry must be *"He must increase, but I must decrease"* (John 3:30). It is a great comfort for me to remember He suffered every temptation I could ever face, yet stood sinless and strong— *"For such a high priest became us, who is holy, harmless, undefiled, separate from sinners, and made higher than the heavens"* (Hebrews 7:26). With His strength, I can do the same, for in Matthew 19:26, He says *"with God all things are possible."* He can help us overcome our selfish desires.

Humility is valuing others higher than ourselves. You probably have already discovered how contrary this is to your natural human tendency! Humility requires an entire transformation of our way of thinking. It is a revolutionary change of mind. If we are critical of others—especially in our thoughts—it is pride. When I begin to think condescending, judgmental, or proud thoughts, I have to simply "tell" my mind to stop and make the choice to harbor uplifting thoughts. When I am tempted to take pride in something I have done, I must purpose to direct all glory to Jesus—remind myself that He is the One who has enabled me to do *anything*; I am nothing on my own. I want to obey the command found in Philippians 2:3, *"Let nothing be done through strife or vainglory; but in lowliness of mind let each esteem other better than themselves."* Guarding my mind requires constant diligence, but eventually the Lord can transform my mind and way of thinking. What a glorious testimony for Christ is the one who deflects all praise to Him and who loves others with His selfless love! This humble attitude truly "provokes" others to good works, as Hebrews 10:24 encourages, *"Let us consider one another to provoke unto love and to good works."*

Jessica Osbebreh, a young missionary wife and mother, shares what the Lord has taught her about true humility—which is much more than our outward actions.

"HUMILITY. I was thirteen and growing in the ways of the Lord when my dad told me, 'I think it will be a struggle for you to learn to be truly humble.' What a shocker! Of all the things he could have said, why humility? If he had told me to be more cheerful or industrious or friendly, yes, I would have had to agree with him... but humility? I thought I had that one down pat! I had always been a naturally shy and quiet person, not one to speak up or blow my own whistle. Was that not what humility was all about? In my mind, humbleness meant quiet, unassuming, meek, and reserved.

"Dad went on to explain, 'Yes, daughter, it will be very hard for you to be humble because you know more than most people about the Bible. You live for the Lord. You're going to have a hard time not looking down on others who have not lived a good life.'

"I marveled at how well Dad had pierced right to the very core of my being. He could not see what was in my heart, but he knew too well the times I had compared myself with others and smugly found myself superior. It was true that I did not watch bad movies, listen to bad music, dress immodestly...the list went on. So I could look at almost anyone else and find some blatant sin in their life; and then, comparing them with my perfect habits, smile inwardly to myself and think, 'You have her/him beat!' I had no idea how badly

CHAPTER SIX — *A Humble Maidservant*

I needed to learn humility.

"Thankfully, I have a loving Dad who was ready to lead me in the quest for humility. We had just met a new family and one of the daughters in the family invited me to give a devotion to a group of her friends that afternoon. Dad suggested I use these verses, Philippians 2:3-5, 'Let nothing be done through strife or vainglory; but in lowliness of mind let each esteem other better than themselves. Look not every man on his own things, but every man also on the things of others. Let this mind be in you, which was also in Christ Jesus.'

"When I started to teach the Word to others, I began understanding it for the first time myself. Humility was not just an outwardly quiet or respectful demeanor; it was to be in my mind and in my heart. I was really supposed to think of others more highly than myself and not to look down upon them. I had the chance to start putting true humility into practice that very day as I led the devotion. One of the girls in the group was very worldly and exactly the sort of person I would have looked down on. As I spoke and glanced around the room familiar thoughts began to play in my mind... *Just look at her...I would never...* Oh no! I realized what I was doing and felt ashamed of myself. *Regard her as more important than yourself,* I told myself to re-think. *It is admirable that she would show interest in the Bible even though she's not from a Christian family. I know I am not a very interesting speaker, but here she is listening to me with such...humility.*

"So I began to learn what it meant to regard others as more important than myself and be truly humble—not on my outward appearance, but in my heart."³

Serving the Lord

The best way we can exemplify Christ's servant attitude is through daily serving our family in our home, in all the "little" ways. My sister, Rachael, is an example of this; she has a servant's heart and loves to help others in need, write notes of encouragement, help Mom make dinner, cook something special for dessert, or play with her siblings. She is always willing to get things for family members or help with the "mundane" tasks. Rachael is especially considerate of family members when they are ill—she is their full-time nurse and will spend her hours caring for them. Through this unselfish attitude, she is learning to demonstrate the attitude of Christ, and she also is encouraging others to serve the Lord as well. I am often inspired by her serving heart!

It is difficult to let go of our selfish desires and serve others. Yet, through these daily opportunities to humbly serve the Lord, God refines our unpolished nature into His beautiful selfless character. Though these "tests" may not be pleasant, we will reap many benefits from them. One night God brought this verse to mind:

> "There hath no temptation taken you but such as is common to man: but God is faithful, who will not suffer you to be tempted above that ye are able; but will with the temptation also make a way to escape, that ye may be able to bear it." (I Corinthians 10:13)

When I awoke, I wondered how this promise could apply to my everyday life. The Lord showed me since He never allows a temptation in my path that cannot be conquered by the grace He provides, there is no reason why I should fail in these trials—I must simply choose to die to self and accept His grace. Through these battles I can learn, trial-by-trial, to relinquish my selfish nature. The wonderful promise of this purging process is that *"when he hath tried me, I shall come forth as gold"* (Job 23:10). I rejoice that God is patient to do this work in my life, and that He will help any who will surrender their pride and selfishness for His work in their life. *"Think it not strange concerning the*

> *"Can any situation* possibly arise, in any circumstance, for which He is not adequate? If He be truly God, there cannot be a single one!"[4]
> —Major W. Ian Thomas

fiery trial which is to try you...but rejoice, inasmuch as ye are partakers of Christ's sufferings" (I Peter 4:12-13).

As we serve our family, we will receive the approval and blessing of God, but by man at times we may be scorned. *"Yea, and all that will live godly in Christ Jesus shall suffer persecution"* (II Timothy 3:12). The world often overlooks the unassuming humble servant, but we must remember who we are trying to please. Whose opinion really matters? Look to Christ's example—He did not seek earthly glory, but let God esteem Him in His perfect time. When the very sinners He was dying for, beat, spat upon, and mockingly hailed Jesus during His crucifixion, He could have right then and there struck them dead. Think of the humility that required! While He was suffering incomprehensible agony as He hung on that cross, Christ could have shown everyone His unlimited power; He could have proved that He *was* truly stronger, that He *was* God. Yet, Christ chose to endure in obedience, so *God* would exalt Him in due time, and so that we could follow His spotless example. *"For there is one God, and one mediator between God and men, the man Christ Jesus; Who gave himself a ransom for all, to be testified in due time"* (I Timothy 2:5-6). Thank you, Jesus!

We should serve others for Christ's sake, not for want of earthly reward. *"Not with eye service, as menpleasers; but as the servants of Christ, doing the will of God from the heart"* (Ephesians 6:6). As we conquer our will in service to the Lord, we will be exalted by God, because He sees each humble act and assures that there is eternal reward in that. James 4:10 says, *"Humble yourselves in the sight of the Lord, and he shall lift you up."* This exaltation is truly more valuable than any earthly praise!

Investing His Talents

"For the body is not one member, but many... If the whole body were an eye, where were the hearing? If the whole were hearing, where were the smelling? But now hath God set the members every one of them in the body, as it hath pleased him." (I Corinthians 12:14-18)

God has blessed each of His children with a gift and talent, but so few use them for their Creator's glory. *"We are the clay, and thou our potter; and we all are the work of thy hand"* (Isaiah 64:8), so we are to esteem Him in every area of life. Using the talents He has bestowed upon us is one way to do this.

First and foremost, we should seek to invest the gifts which the Lord has bestowed upon us right in our home, to further our parent's vision. This is when we will be most productive—when we, as daughters, incorporate our skills to complement our family's talents and father's vision. For example, I enjoy singing and harmonizing, more so than the rest of my family; thus I wondered why God gave me these interests, until my mom pointed out that I can *teach* my family to harmonize. I am now helping my brothers learn their parts, in hopes that someday we all will be able to harmonize together. I can use this gift from God to help my family work together. How vibrant is the family unit when each individual is using their talent in an unified effort! We know several families who play instruments together and minister to the elderly through their music. If each family member did not invest their talent into this, it would not be possible. Other friends produce godly resources for families, and each member has a part in the ministry—working together to impact the world for the glory of God. I Corinthians 12:14 explains that *"the body is not one member, but many."*

Seek to apply your gifts in your family. If your spiritual gift is encouragement, start today encouraging your siblings to read the Word with you each morning. If it is serving, then start this hour helping your mom with the laundry, cooking, and cleaning. The Lord wants to find us faithful in the small tasks, before He will promote us to tasks of more responsibility. *"Because thou hast been faithful in a very little, have thou* authority over ten cities" (Luke 19:17). The Lord will judge us according to what we have been given and how we use it for His glory; Luke 12:48 says, *"For unto whomsoever much is given, of him shall be much required: and to whom men have committed much, of him they will ask the more."*

> *"I have found in my* own life that when I am pursuing my father's goals, my own gifts and abilities fall beautifully into place. But when my personal goals are placed first in my life, the right things are not done."
>
> —Elisha Wahlquist (21), Daughter at Home

As Blessings to Others

Matthew 25 tells the parable of the servants who were given talents. Jesus said those who invested their money were wise, but one servant who felt his earnings were insignificant decided to bury his talents. When his master returned, this servant was asked for a report of his talents, but his foolish reply was inadequate: *"Lord, I knew thee that thou art a hard man...and I was afraid, and went and hid thy talent in the earth: lo, there thou hast that is thine"* (vs. 24-5).

God desires us to use the talents He has bestowed upon us to glorify Him, not to hide and waste them. Indeed, if we do not apply them, they will waste away—*"from him that hath not shall be taken away even that which he hath"* (vs. 29). Years ago, Mom was shown she had the gift of discernment, and can attest to the fact that if she does not practice this gift, she will lose her ability to discern.

The Lord calls us to use the talents He has bestowed upon us in different ways, but the goal remains the same—to bring Him glory. We must keep our eyes open for opportunities to bless others as He leads. *"As every man hath received the gift, even so minister the same one to another, as good stewards of the manifold grace of God"* (I Peter 4:10).

The Lord has given me a desire to encourage Christian girls. As I have shared earlier, when I was younger, I felt very alone in my convictions. It also seemed that few older girls were interested in my life. About this time, God provided godly fellowship and encouragement for me through a magazine for Christian young women. It inspired me to start my own publication for the encouragement of other girls. My parents were supportive and helped me lay out and print the first little issue of *The King's Blooming Rose* magazine. This outreach has grown over the past five years, and today hundreds of young ladies across the globe receive *KBR*. I feel so unworthy of the great responsibility God has bestowed on me in this ministry, yet how blessed I am by it. The Lord has taught me the importance of serving others and using the gifts He has blessed me with. I have also been tremendously blessed to meet many other Christian girls through *KBR*.

> "Whether you have much or little natural [talent], there is reason for its cultivation and room for its use. Place it at your Lord's disposal, and He will show you how to make the most of it for Him."[5]
> —Francis Havergal (1879)

The ministry that has first priority in life is our relationship with God and our family. We can do a good thing at the wrong time. We must prioritize, making sure other projects do not take time away from our family responsibilities. We must focus on the duties at home before we seek to bless those outside our home. I have found it important to ask myself questions before working on some projects,

— Have I done all I can to help my family before I work on this?
— Is there a need in the family I can fulfill right now?
— Does the Lord have another task for me to before I do this?

As I sit down at my computer to write, I try to ask myself, "Am I pleasing Jesus by working on this project right now? Or is there something else more important that I need to do?" At times, the Lord puts on my heart a task that is more eternally important—such as assisting my sister do her chores, helping Mom iron, or talking with my brother for a few minutes. When I do whatever the Lord prompted me to do and come back to write, I know I have done the Lord's will—and He will be able to use me more effectively because my priorities are in order.

It is wonderful to use our talents for God's glory, but we must be sure to keep this as our focus; this has been a struggle for me to remember. It is all too easy to become so focused on the work in some good "ministry" that I forget He is using me as *His* instrument. My attitude should be—"How can God use me in this ministry He has given me? How can I bring more glory to Him?" I also have to remember to place my father's vision over any other area—

– Have I completed all projects that Dad has asked or would like me to do? Do I delay in finishing tasks for him?
– Are all my duties in the family business complete?
– Am I doing my best in what I do for Dad, or am I rushing in those projects to work on other plans?

Ways to Invest Talents

Ask God how He wants to use your talent to bless others. Be willing to obey His direction, and let Him use you as His vessel. Always remember you are His clay and follow His leading. There are endless opportunities to reach out to others as a blessing. Here are a few ideas:

– **Music:** Use your musical talents to bless the elderly or your church members. You could also encourage people by recording God-glorifying music; I have been tremendously blessed by uplifting songs one of my friends wrote and recorded. Develop your vocal ability by singing along with a recording of acappella hymns; for a greater challenge, learn to harmonize. I learned to sing harmony by singing with recordings. Vocal instructional books are also helpful if no teacher is available. Even if you think you do not have any musical talent, Psalm 98:4 in-

structs us to *"make a joyful noise unto the* LORD...*rejoice, and sing praise."* The Lord is glorified through our efforts to praise Him.[6]

- **Sewing Services**: This is an invaluable skill for any girl to be proficient in, especially since modest clothing is often difficult to find. The ability to design and sew your family's clothes can be a great blessing for your family and future family. You can bless others by sewing modest clothing for mothers who do not have time to sew for themselves or their daughters.

- **Nutritious Cooking**: Start now blessing your family by taking responsibility for planning and cooking your family's meals. This will not only lighten your mom's load, but it will also help you learn to cook well-balanced and nutrient-dense meals. I know two sisters, ages sixteen and eighteen, who undertook cooking meals for their family. They take turns each week, planning menus and cooking nutritious food. Home-cooked meals are a wonderful way to bless and comfort others; be a blessing by preparing a meal for someone sick, a family who has a new baby, or for a busy mother.

- **Warm Hospitality**: Hospitality is important to the Lord, and can be used as a dynamic tool in witnessing to others. *"Use hospitality one to another without grudging"* (I Peter 4:9). Support your father's hospitality; when he invites company over, make it a pleasant memory for your guests. Do your part in tidying up the home and making it cheerful and cozy, and when your guests arrive, warmly greet them. I particularly remember the hospitality one family showed to us when we visited them while we were traveling, and how welcome they made us feel. When we arrived, their family rushed outside and warmly greeted us with hearty hugs and handshakes. My friend led me inside, offered to sit my things down, inquired about our trip, and made me feel at home. We spent a relaxing night around the fireplace talking, singing, reading the Bible, and playing music. The children considerately put us first when serving our plates or asking what activities we would like to do. Be considerate of your guests' interests, as well as their parents' desires, by asking their parents if they allow the activities you have planned.

— Godly Encouragement:

Through Letters—I have found letter-writing a great way to encourage young girls in need of a friend. Write not only younger girls, striving to encourage them in the Lord, but also godly older girls, who can inspire you to grow, as well. This ministry can be tackled anywhere—whenever you have time, paper and a pen.

Through Writing—You can write articles encouraging others in godliness, sharing these in magazines or other resources.

Through Contact—Be an encouragement to those around you, especially younger girls. This is incredibly important and can change lives. I cannot tell you how much it has meant to me when older girls have shown an interest in my life and spiritual growth. I look for those who have gone ahead of me in their Christian walk and who are willing to impart wisdom. I cannot stress enough how powerful it can be to simply befriend younger sisters in Christ.

Through Church—One very important ministering opportunity can be found right in your church. You should make a point to bless other church members and go out of your way to welcome visitors. My family has visited several churches throughout the years. One thing that has stood out during these visits, is the way the young people of the church have acted—many times they were "too busy" to acknowledge our presence. In contrast, at another church we visited, a line of young people greeted visitors as they arrived at the door, shaking hands and cheerfully welcoming others into the church. What a blessing it was to enter this fellowship on that Sunday morning—to see smiling faces who were happy for us to join their congregation and worship the Lord together. One young lady in particular was so sweet and led us to seats, made sure we had hymnals, and made our family feel so welcome. Her selflessness and servant's heart has been an incredible example in my life. She has demonstrated to me the impact of the serving role a daughter can have both in her home and in the Church. Thank you, Susanna! Young ladies, you do not realize how much of an impact you make as an ambassador of the Bride of Christ; use this opportunity for Christ's glory.

Areas in which we can serve and bless others surround us; we simply need to keep our eyes open and have a heart turned toward the needs of others in our church and community. Young women can be bright lights of godliness to their world simply because they have decided to glorify the Lord—to serve someone besides themselves. A life lived for the Lord will have a tremendous impact. Let us seek to humbly reach out to others, for the sake of our Lord Jesus. "*He that is greatest among you shall be your servant. And whosoever shall exalt himself shall be abased; and he that shall humble himself shall be exalted*" (Matthew 23:11-12).

CHAPTER SIX ~ *A Humble Maidservant*

on my shelf... RELATED RESOURCES

-- *Jessie Wells* and the *Ester Reid Series* by Mrs. Isabella Alden (Keepers of the Faith, P.O. Box 100, Ironwood, MI 49938; *www.keepersofthefaith.com*)

-- *Keepers At Home* by Jennie Chandler (Author House, 1663 Liberty Drive Suite 200, Bloomington, IN 47403, 800.839.8640; *www.authorhouse.com*)

-- *The God of All Comfort* by Hannah Whitall Smith (Moody Publishers, 820 N. LaSalle Boulevard, Chicago, IL 60610; *www.moodypublishing.com*)

-- *The Little Preacher* by Mrs. Elizabeth Prentiss (HSM Publishing, 92-594 Palpailai St., Kapolei, HI 96707; *www.hsmpublishing.com*)

-- *Flowers From A Puritan's Garden* by C.H. Spurgeon (Sprinkle Publications, P.O. Box 1094, Harrisonburg, VA 22801)

-- *Streams in the Desert* by L.B. Cowman (Zondervan, Grand Rapids, MI 49530)

-- *Verses of Virtue* compiled by Mrs. Beall Phillips (The Vision Forum Inc., 4719 Blanco Road, San Antonio, TX 76212; *www.visionforum.com*)

-- *The Imitation of Christ* by Thomas à Kempis (Moody Publishers, 820 N. LaSalle Boulevard, Chicago, IL 60610; *www.moodypublishing.com*)

"Be subject one to another, & be clothed with *humility*:
for God resisteth the proud, and **giveth grace** to the humble.
Humble yourselves therefore under the mighty hand of God,
that he may exalt you in due time:
Casting all your care upon him; for he careth for you."
—I PETER 5:5-7

a family daughter...
JOANNA DUKA

THE LORD HAS blessed me with a wonderful home and family, for whom I have always been grateful. However, it was not until recently that I understood the role of a daughter in the home and the special purpose she fulfills serving in it. I have a great interest in politics and had plans for what I hoped would be a career in government. I found it to be a way to fight for the issues in which I believe. I was looking forward to graduating, and going to college to earn a degree that would be bring me closer to achieving my goal.

However, I began to feel frustrated. I found my plan was conflicted by certain Scriptures which instructed women not to be in authority over men: *"But I would have you know, that the head of every man is Christ; and the head of the woman is the man; and the head of Christ is God"* (I Corinthians 11:3; see also I Timothy 2:11,12). I tried to figure out some way I could hold elected office and still be in accordance with Scripture. I wanted to be a mother someday, but wanted to do something important as a single person as well. The Lord began to gently prepare my heart to embrace a better path. At a homeschool convention, I bought the Botkins's book, *So Much More*. I began reading it and became uncomfortable with the concepts. However, I continued reading and the Lord used the book to inspire me through Scripture to show me another calling, that is so wonderful that I was immediately ready to give up my other plans.

Being a daughter at home no longer seemed like an ordinary or boring station, but something with purpose! I suddenly realized there was meaning in tasks like washing dishes and doing laundry. There were siblings to love, a mom to help and learn from, and a father to respect and serve. I found new ways to serve my father and began looking for opportunities to further his mission. I had to begin with the very small things, but even those small areas can be a great blessing to a father. The Lord brought an even greater opportunity to assist my father, who is a pastor. When his secretary was unable to continue her work, I was able to take on her responsibilities to lighten his load. When Dad could not find a greeter on Sunday mornings, the Lord gave me the opportunity to do it.

I also have opportunities to serve my mother and siblings. I enjoy cooking dinner several times a week, doing morning devotions with my younger brothers, and teaching my younger sister preschool. I am now looking forward to graduating so I can help my mom school my siblings and take responsibility for more of the housework. I am truly grateful to the Lord for each opportunity He has brought me to serve others.

I want more than anything to be a mother someday; by fulfilling this role I truly can be influential in raising up a generation for Christ—not in taking over the man's role to lead in government. I am still new on this journey as a daughter preparing to be a keeper at home, and continue to learn every day by His grace. I am so grateful!

JOANNA DUKA (15) *lives with her family in Phoenix, Arizona, where her father is a pastor and her mother is a homemaker. She has two younger brothers and two younger sisters. She enjoys reading, playing the piano, cooking and baking. She desires to live her life for the Lord.*

"*Lord,*

In place of all the joys of the world
grant me the sweet anointing of your Spirit,
and instead of the loves of this life,
pour in the *love of your name.*"[1]

[THOMAS À KEMPIS]

"*Let* the *beauty*
OF THE LORD OUR GOD
be *upon us.*"

[PSALM 90:17]

CHAPTER SEVEN

THE *Spotless* MAIDEN

MOST GIRLS DESIRE to look beautiful. In Christ, every girl *can* be beautiful—because a life lived apart from the world and dwelling in Him is the most beautiful, rare gem to behold.² Inward beauty is a trait that we, as daughters of the King of purity, should seek wholeheartedly.

The Lord is beautiful and holy, and commands us to be likewise: *"For God hath not called us unto uncleanness, but unto holiness"* (I Thessalonians 4:7). We must focus on inward purity of heart because this is what truly matters in the sight of God. I Samuel 16:7 says, *"The Lord seeth not as man seeth...the Lord looketh on the heart."*

How do we seek this beauty? When we embrace the plan the Lord has for us as daughters, our lives will radiate God's peace and joy. I have seen girls who are beautiful because they love the calling the Lord has given them, and they delight in their femininity. They are serene, radiant, joyful, happy, content, and satisfied.

The feminist movement in our society has affected the ambitions of women. Many girls fight against anything to do with being feminine. Most women think that when they act ladylike, they display weakness; yet they will not find fulfillment when they reject God's plan. As Christians, we must refute this mentality and accept God's beautiful plan for us. When we embrace God's will, what fulfillment and satisfaction we will find! Our hearts will abide in the perfect peace of God.

Distinct Roles

God has given men and women different roles, and we should not try to fill the role of the other, but instead assist and complement them. As women, we do not need to prove ourselves physically "strong" or equal to men, but rather fulfill the role as help-meet while exercising the inward strength described in I Peter 3:4, *"Let it be the hidden man of the heart, in that which is not corruptible, even the ornament of a meek and quiet spirit, which is in the sight of God of great price."*

Women have great influence in a culture. As daughters, we impact many lives through the choices we make. If you do not think serving the Lord in your home is of much importance, you are missing so much! Our God works through those who are faithfully fulfilling His commandments—*no matter* what the majority is doing. *"I will gather the remnant of my flock...and they shall be fruitful and increase"* (Jeremiah 23:3). This has been such a comforting reminder to me; it is a blessing to know that the Lord sees the few who are following Him, even if millions of others in this perverse generation choose otherwise. God can greatly use our faithfulness; fulfilling our mission is extremely important.

> "The secret weapon for transforming the culture at large, and equipping the church...is the availability of virtuous women committed to fulfilling their God-appointed roles."[3]

Because we want to take joy in the calling the Lord has given us as girls, we should not display a "tomboy" attitude. This has been an area of struggle in my life, especially when I was younger and enjoyed rough, boyish activities. There was nothing wrong with these things by themselves, but I displayed a competitive and feministic attitude toward boys when I participated in them. If climbing trees, arm wrestling, or other activities which often pertain to men caused me to act unladylike, it is probably best for me to avoid them. I also try to avoid competing with my brothers in any way. I want to encourage them to be manly by acting like a lady, not trying to take over their domains of interest. My friend Elisha shares her testimony,

> "In my early teens, I enjoyed running, especially since God had given me a gift of speed. A game of tag would often end up with me racing the fastest boy who was playing. It was innocent fun—yet, as I grew older, I began to realize that God was not glorified by it. He created women to be the help-meet of men, not to compete with them. When a girl or a lady is competitive with men, they lose their respect for her, and begin to treat her like they treat each other—and women ultimately lose in that kind of a contest. That is the lie of feminism, the lie that women should be able to take over the dominions that God has given to man."

We should strive to encourage men in their role as well. As ladies, we can encourage men to be manly by graciously accepting their assistance, such as opening the door for us or letting us go ahead of them in line. We should delight in receiving help from men who exemplify Christ in protecting the weaker vessel (I Peter 3:7). There have been instances when I have turned down my brother's or another man's assistance before thinking, and I regret those lost opportunities. Recently, I was unloading our grocery cart into our van. I had some paper towels in my hand, when my brother offered to load them for me. Before I had stopped to think, I replied, "No thanks, I have it!" Immediately, I felt remorseful of my answer, for I should have accepted his offer even if I truly had not needed it. It is common for women to reject a man's assistance with the attitude, "I am capable of doing it all myself and do not need *your* help!" They do not want to be treated as if they are not able to do what a man can do. We do not have to compete with men to prove ourselves capable. We must constantly remind ourselves of our God-given role—which although distinct from man's, is not inferior—so we do *not* discourage the masculinity of men.

Since the Fall of mankind, submission to authority has been a struggle for women.[4] I know in my own life this has been hard; I have to continually learn to submit to my authority, and to embrace my dad's vision. This is often hard because I do not want to relinquish my own will. My sinful, self-willed nature is hideous to behold; something with God's help, I desire to overcome.

Distinct Femininity

We should seek to dress and act in a manner that brings our heavenly Father and earthly father a good name and honorable reputation, because we are their ambassadors. Our appearance will give the first and most lasting impression to others. Observe yourself in the mirror—does your attire stand out or draw attention to yourself? Is it conveying the right message? Does it honor your authorities? Are you carrying yourself in a feminine, modest way in your posture, manners, and actions?

Feminine and distinct clothing is important; we must dress in a way that is becoming to our role as women. We should not undermine this calling by trying to dress as men; the Lord tells us to dress distinctly: "*The woman shall not wear that which pertaineth unto a man, neither shall a man put on a woman's garment: for all that do so are abomination unto the* LORD *thy God*" (Deuteronomy 22:5). This emphasizes the differences in the callings the Lord has given men and women. Delight in wearing feminine colors and styles!

A neat appearance is imperative to being a good witness for Christ. Every girl, no matter what her family's dress standard is, can apply basic principles in the area of maintaining clean, orderly and neat dress. Our God is a God of order, as I Corinthians 14:40 instructs, *"Let all things be done decently and in order."* While there may be certain dirty tasks when we need to dress accordingly, we do not need to habitually appear in public with an unorganized, shuffled appearance. It is worth changing that dirty shirt before going on errands—you never know who He may bring across your path—the Lord may have a witnessing opportunity for you!

Honoring Dress

I Timothy 2:9 instructs women to dress modestly: *"In like manner also, that women adorn themselves in modest apparel, with shamefacedness and sobriety."* Since a young age, my parents have taught me the importance of dressing in orderly and modest clothing. At times I have wanted to wear something they have not approved of, and have thought, *What is the harm of wearing this dress which is a bit tighter? It is only one time!* But the Lord has shown me the importance of evaluating my wardrobe to fit my authorities' preferences, not just their requirements. It is always worth the "sacrifice" when I honor my parents in this way. It is not always easy to do this; I have to make sure I am truly dressing in a way that pleases my father, not someone I might want to impress. One friend shared that she had been through the same struggles of honoring her parents' dress code, so her father would check her clothing before each outing, and if necessary he asked her to change a part of her outfit that was inappropriate. Until she learned to honor him in her clothing choices, he carefully protected her in this way.

Your parents' clothing preferences for you may be very different from what is the secular style. It can be difficult at times to dress differently from what others are wearing or is "the current fashion." Yet, we are called to be a light to the world (Matthew 5:14) not of the world (Romans 12:2). I encourage you to not worry about what others—even your friends—wear. This is difficult to do, but remind yourself, *I have to remember that what is important for me as a daughter, is making sure I dress in accordance with my family's standard.* As you simply honor this standard, your example will also be a testimony to others, including siblings, friends, acquaintances, and younger girls.

If you are in question of some particular clothing, I encourage you to ask your mom or dad if they like it, and also pay attention to remarks they make about certain clothes—these are indicators of their preferences. I know it may be hard to surrender your preferences, but it is our duty to submit (Exodus 20:12), and remember that the Lord will bless your obedience!

Modest Dress

It is vital that we keep in mind the true meaning of modesty in our clothing choices. *Webster's 1828 Dictionary* describes "modest" as, "Moderate; not excessive or extreme; not extravagant." Often we think, "the more clothing, the better," yet this is not necessarily the truth—when excessive, it is by definition, *not* modest. Modest clothing is moderate and does not draw attention to itself. In striving to dress modestly and femininely, sometimes I have found myself taking things too far. When I began sewing clothes years ago, I enjoyed learning to style my own clothing. Since my parents want my skirts to be modest, I make them long. At one point I designed a style that was extremely long and full. It was soon after I began wearing these skirts, that I realized they were no longer truly modest—looking in the mirror, what was the focal point? They were attention-grabbing; they drew more attention to myself than was necessary. I have found that there are skirts of sufficient length and fullness to be modest, without attracting attention. I desire my clothing to be meek and moderate—not conspicuous like a neon-orange sports car with no muffler zipping through town.

Any part of our clothing can be taken to an extreme. Let us follow our parents' advice and dress in a truly modest, gentle, pure, and unassuming manner—pointing to the One who reigns in our heart.

Pure Dress

Our clothing should direct others to Jesus, not to ourselves. Do not let your outward appearance overtake your thoughts; remember that the *heart* matters too. Seek to bring glory to Christ alone, and guard to make sure your motives are pure. God sees your true intent. A friend, Rebecca Serven Loomis, encouraged me,

> "KEEP IN MIND, dear girls, that while man looks on the outward appearance, the Lord looks on the heart. You know your heart; are you seeking to be modest and feminine? Praise God! This is a glorious thing to embrace God's design as a woman. On the other hand, are you focusing on the outward at the neglect of the hidden man of the heart? A meek and quiet spirit is acceptable in the sight of God.
>
> "We should not let our beauty be based in outward adornment, as in the braiding of hair, the beautiful garments we wear, or of our outward appearance. Rather, let it be based on our relationship with the Lord: the joy we have in our heart because of His work in our lives... I want to keep growing in this area—and there are so many other things I pray the Lord will continue to grow in my life! Dearest girls, I pray the Lord helps you to reflect a picture of beautiful womanhood—from the inside and out."

Press towards His beautiful holiness by delighting in Him and shining forth His joy through your honorable dress!

Daily Dress

I met a young lady a few years ago who wore feminine clothing and had a clean, orderly appearance. I wondered what clothing she would wear every day at home, and I was not surprised by her reply:

"I just wear the same things [around home] that I wear everywhere else. I try to dress beautifully and femininely whether others will see me, or just my family. Wearing a clean, pressed dress or jumper with a nice blouse and keeping your hair orderly and brushed may seem to be an extra pain when only your family will be seeing you, but it makes quite a difference in your attitude, and shows your family that they are just as important as strangers outside."

Since it is easy for me to fall into the habit of wearing "old clothes" around my home, I was encouraged by her words to try it myself. I found it does not take much extra time to make sure I had a fresh appearance—even "just for my family." When I made an extra effort to look nice daily, it proved to be a blessing to myself as well, because I looked at my family in a new perspective. If I was going to dress nicely for them, I also treated them with respect.

Untainted by the World

A maiden of the Lord strives to remain pure in Christ, as Psalm 45:13 so beautifully states, *"The king's daughter is all glorious within."* We must protect our minds and hearts for our pure Bridegroom and for our future husband. The biblical example of a man and woman preparing for the covenant of marriage is a far cry from the regular dating game accepted by our society. My parents are committed to guiding and protecting me until the Lord brings a life partner into my life. I desire to keep my heart pure for that one man, as did Isaac for his wife Rebekah in Genesis 24. While I think we girls should be excited about the idea of God's providential provision of our future mate, it should not constantly fill our thought-life. Marriage should not be our life goal; we need to focus on the Lord Jesus and His Kingdom. Plus, if we are always dreaming about the future, we will be disappointed when the time comes because our expectations will be too high. I encourage you to trust your heart to God so you can commit a *complete* heart to your husband someday, if the Lord so wills. If you trust Him to save you from hell through Christ, then in comparison, providing a mate for you is a small matter for the Lord to accomplish! Remember this, and guard your heart until then.

I know this can be easier said than done. Even though I have entrusted my future to the Lord, I have found that it can still be hard to focus on the Lord and not wonder at times about the future. Many girls express the same struggle to keep their focus on Christ. Recently, the Lord showed me that one reason I worried about my future was because I had a distorted view of singleness. My focus was more on future marriage, than the mission God has for me *today*. There is a season for everything, and I had been overlooking the season at hand while dreaming of the future. *"To every thing there is a season, and a time to every purpose under the heaven"* (Ecclesiastes 3:1).

Grace for Each Season

When I was a young girl, because I looked forward to marriage very much, the thought that God might not have that for me until "later" in life was an overwhelming fear of mine. It seemed

> *"If a young woman* is dreaming of the future in discontentment, she will continue to be discontent when married. If she is not content with her father and Jesus, she will not be content with a husband and Jesus."
>
> —Thomas Bryant

that if this was His plan for me, it would be unbearable. Yet, through the past several years, the Lord has shown me the purpose for this season of life as an unmarried girl. I have also realized that I can choose to be content in whatever season God has me in, and that His will for my life are never "unbearable"! They are always good—"*For I know the thoughts that I think toward you, saith the* Lord, *thoughts of peace, and not of evil*" (Jeremiah 29:11). Furthermore, God gives sufficient grace for each day that He will guide us through; "*My grace is sufficient for thee: for my strength is made perfect in weakness*" (II Corinthians 12:9). One friend admitted that if she had known when she was younger that she would still be single in her thirties, she probably would not have been able to bear the thought. The Lord mercifully spared her that knowledge, and as she has followed the Lord one day at a time, she testified that His grace has always been sufficient for each hour.

I have spoken with older unmarried girls about contentment and finding fulfillment in their father's home as "singles." These young ladies have shared the importance of making *Christ* their all. One girl shared a very profound point that proved to be a tremendous blessing on my outlook of marriage. I remarked that it is difficult to understand why some girls get married young, while others, who in my opinion seem better prepared, have to wait for many years to marry. She said,

> "I do not think it is about how 'prepared' we are. Marriage is not a 'level' we reach, as if we are not as useful to God now as we are when married. We are all useful when we are in the center of His will. God may take each through stages of life at different times to teach them lessons in different ways."

That was a new thought to me! I realized I had unconsciously thought of marriage as my ultimate goal—that until I was married, I was not really "living life" or as useful to God. I almost viewed my unmarried years as unimportant, as simply "waiting." In a word, I was discontent. As I began to see this season at home as important as marriage itself, because this was the Lord's plan for my life, I became incredibly excited! I began to see that I had such a rich oasis of opportunity right now to invest in my family. I became content to abide here, fulfilled in His plan. I now praise the Lord with every fiber in my being that He has me here in my home, and I desire to use these days fruitfully in service and growth. God can use us wherever we are in life—single or married, young or old, weak or strong; we simply need to realize and accept this.

God's plan and timing for each of His children is different. He may teach one girl to trust Him by waiting for a husband, while at the same time He may teach another girl who is already married to rely on Him through a different struggle. God has a different plan for everyone; as one friend put it, "that makes being His child so exciting"! There will always be something to wait on and trust God for, and the sooner we learn these lessons, the sooner we can move on to the next lesson, my Mom says. Delight in your days at home and *fill them* to the brim. Do not think, "I'm *waiting* for 'real life' to begin when I get married [or whatever your dream may be]."

Love Enough, Love Overflowing

We should never put anyone or anything above God in our lives. "*Thou shalt have no other gods before me*" (Exodus 20:3). Most of us would never do that purposefully, but many of us do it unknowingly. How many times have you thought, *If only I could do____, I would feel fulfilled!* Or, *If____ was standing by my side right now, I would be so happy.* I know I am not guiltless in this area! Whatever this envious longing may be in our life, we elevate it higher than God in our heart when we think these thoughts; thus, we break the first commandment.

This is easier to do this than it might seem. How many of us truly love our Lord higher than *any* thing, *any* goal, or *any* person in this world? Is our ultimate goal, our deepest longing, and our heart's cry to love Jesus more? Are we willing to give up any deep desire for Jesus?

Everything on earth will pass away; only eternal things will last. The only relationship that will last throughout all eternity is with our

Creator—our Savior. When I think of life with this outlook, I wonder in amazement at what a fool I am to want to invest time in anything besides Him, why I ever desire anything above Him, and why would I seek anything less than an inseparable friendship with Him.

God commands us to love Him *"with all thy heart, and with all thy soul, and with all thy mind,"* in Matthew 22:37. We *must* realize that only God can fulfill all of the deep longings of our heart—no human can fill that place. Christ is the only One who will never change nor fail us and He always knows what we are feeling.

I have been realizing the great importance of making Jesus my closest friend. Several years ago I thought, *That is only for super-spiritual people! I don't know how to love Jesus that much. Practically, how can you do that?* The Lord has been showing me how He *can* be my best, constant friend, and this truly has been a rich blessing.

This *can* be reality in your life. You may ask, "How do I make Jesus my closest friend?" Actually the answer is very simple. How do you get to know anyone better whom you love? How do you deepen your relationship with any friend? You would talk with them often and share what has happened in your life. You probably share your heart, concerns, struggles, desires, and all the little events of life. It is the same way with our relationship with Jesus. He understands everything we face— He bore these trials, too. We can invest in this relationship just as we would an earthly friend—only more deeply, earnestly, wholeheartedly and openly! We should talk with Jesus unceasingly, share our heart with Him, listen to Him through His Word, repent of our sins against Him, pour out

> *"Emotional freedom* is not the absence of a desire for marriage or indifference toward young men. Rather it is the liberty to love the Lord wholeheartedly & without distraction."[5]
> —Molly Cassidy (23), Daughter at Home

CHAPTER SEVEN — *The Spotless Maiden*

our longings at His feet, and ask Him to lead us in all situations. During your day, share with Christ your feelings and struggles as an on-going conversation. When you are struggling with certain impure thoughts, turn them right over to your Savior—"Lord Jesus, I give this thought over to you." Use these struggles to turn to Him in prayer. Give Him the place in your heart that you would give the closest Friend.

As women, we have a desire to be loved. In the marriage relationship this is partly fulfilled by the husband, but Jesus is the only One who can completely fulfill this desire. An older girl shared with me from personal experience that she realized no man would be able to fulfill all of her spiritual needs and emotional desires. She encouraged me to seek the Lord for these fulfillments now. Often we girls tend to think "prince charming" will fill every desire, and that after he comes along, life will be perfectly peachy. Do you hope for a husband to fill your longings, to love you? Do you see areas in your relationship with Christ that need growth, but you ignore them thinking, *When I am married it will not matter?* If so, you will be greatly disappointed. We will love our husbands and be fulfilled in them only in proportion with the deepness of the relationship we have with our heavenly Bridegroom. When we have found complete fulfillment in Christ alone, all other earthly joys will be "an added blessing." Isaiah 54:4 vividly describes the all-sufficiency of our Maker—"*For thy Maker is thine husband; the* Lord *of hosts is his name; and thy Redeemer the Holy One of Israel; The God of the whole earth shall he be called.*"

Sister, I encourage you to make a commitment to ardently invest in this relationship with your Creator; it will be one you will never regret. It will set you emotionally free as you fully serve Him. When we choose to invest in this all-important relationship with Jesus and pour out our hearts to Him, our lives will be radiant with His love. By surrendering our deepest desires, committing ourselves to love the Lord with our entire heart, and trusting Him to fulfill our needs, we will become a beautiful beacon of Christ because of our emotional freedom. The choice is yours. Will you remove anything that is between you and your Savior? Will you enjoy His rich fellowship, His calming presence? This is a choice which will not only impact your own life, but also your family—and ultimately the world around you.

Focus on the Kingdom

There was a time when I was fearful about how to act around young men; in striving to avoid being forward—but rather "shamefaced" and reserved as the Bible tells women to be in I Timothy 2:9—I became so self-conscious that I actually drew attention to myself.

We must focus on the Kingdom of God and desire to point others to Christ, because *"every one of us shall give account of himself to God"* (Romans 14:12). If we are seeking Christ's glory and have an eternal perspective of His Kingdom, our focus will be right, and in turn, our actions toward young men will be appropriate. We will want to treat them as fellow laborers in the Kingdom, not distract them. I certainly do not want to cause any young man to stumble in his walk with the Lord. The Lord has shown me that instead of acting self-consciously around young men or even ignoring them, I should be courteous, respectful, honorable, and natural—yet discreet. I need to treat them as *men*, as my brothers in Christ. When we ladies treat young men with all respect as we would an older church elder, it will be so much easier for us to guard our hearts and for young men to focus on the Lord. *"Rebuke not an elder, but entreat him as a father; and the younger men as brethren"* (I Timothy 5:1). Our heart attitude really shows through our actions!

In dealing with young men, I must keep their best interest in mind just as I do my own brothers'. I think of it this way—*how would I want another girl to treat my brother?* Just as I strive to protect them from temptations, in the same way, I should want to protect the purity of

CHAPTER SEVEN — *The Spotless Maiden*

other young men. While we should regard young men as brothers in the Lord, that does not mean that we should treat them as we treat *our own* brothers, or be as familiar as with our girl friends. We should still be respectful and chaste, meaning "innocent, clean, perfect."[6]

Seek your parents' counsel and keep your relationship with them open. At this point, we should invest in relationships with our parents and older "Titus Two" women to glean from their wisdom. We must keep our thoughts focused on Jesus, and as we do so, seek the company of the wise and more mature. *"He that walketh with wise men shall be wise: but a companion of fools shall be destroyed"* (Proverbs 13:20).

Victory of the Mind

When we deal with young men as brothers in all purity, it will help us keep our minds focused on the Lord, and being fulfilled in Him, waiting for His timing to bring marriage into our life. Yet, there probably will be times when we feel an attraction to a young man. These feelings and thoughts must not be allowed a foothold in our minds; II Timothy 2:22 warns us, *"Flee also youthful lusts: but follow righteousness, faith, charity, peace, with them that call on the Lord out of a pure heart."* II Corinthians 10:5 says we should be *"casting down imaginations...and bringing into captivity every thought to the obedience of Christ."* In obedience to these commands, we must simply *choose* to flee these temptations. Guarding our hearts is a *constant*, repetitive choice. Won't it be worth it though, to be brought to the marriage alter as a spotless maiden, with a pure testimony before Christ and man? *"Pure religion and undefiled before God and the Father is this...to keep him-*

More Love to Thee!

More love to Thee, O Christ,
More love to Thee!
Hear Thou the prayer I make
On bended knee.
This is my earnest plea:
More love, O Christ, to Thee.

—Elizabeth Prentiss (1856)

self unspotted from the world" (James 1:27).

When a thought comes into my mind that is not pure, I must turn to the Lord in prayer. I have to apply the fruits of the Spirit, self-control and patience: *"But the fruit of the Spirit is...longsuffering...and temperance"* (Galatians 5:22). I must not allow myself to grow discontent by entertaining longings of things that I do not have, so in prayer I give Christ the desires I am feeling. Once we make a disciplined habit of choosing the right and refuting the wrong, God will grant victory in our thought-life!

There are times when I struggle with these emotions throughout the day; sometimes it becomes incredibly difficult to altogether avoid these thoughts. During times like this, it helps me to write "letters" to Jesus and share my feelings with Him that way. It is a relief to pour out my feelings to Him. God's Word says in Psalm 62:8, *"Pour out your heart before him: God is a refuge for us."* This has become a comforting verse to me. As I learn to place my deep desires and struggles at His feet, I am refreshed by the refuge I find in His holy presence!

An Open Heart

Another thing that helps me when I find myself struggling with thoughts towards a young man, is to consider *their* well-being. If they are unsaved, I pray that we as a family might be used as an instrument to point to their lost state before Him. If they are saved and lives display godly character traits, I thank God for their example and pray that their walk with the Lord will not be hindered by the temptations of the world. It is important that I then turn my mind in prayer to the needs of other people and situations. Sarah Mally, in her book *Before You Meet Prince Charming*, adds, "The enemy is going to think twice about stirring up vain thoughts when he realizes that every time the thought comes, you simply turn it into a prayer."[8] My dad has encouraged me to discipline my mind in this area, because these feelings will not just "go away"

CHAPTER SEVEN — *The Spotless Maiden*

later when I am married. It will be a choice I will have to make then as well—I will have to choose to be loyal to my own husband and turn away thoughts of others.

An important step in remaining pure is to share our struggles with our parents. We should be thankful for the tremendous blessing of having parents who care for our purity and well-being. It can be hard to expose these deep feelings with those who know us so well, but it truly is worth it. In the past, when I have shared my feelings with my parents, I have been amazed at how understanding they are. I had no idea they had already noticed the areas I struggled with, and they were glad for me to share my heart with them.

I encourage you to share with your parents the issues laying on your heart before it becomes an emotional burden in your life. I have waited to talk with my mom and dad about situations that have bothered me, hoping my feelings would just go away. As time passed, the burden only became heavier, and I became downhearted by these worries. When I finally shared my burden with my parents, I felt great freedom!

Friends who have encouraged me to share my heart with my parents have testified that each time they talked with their parents, it becomes easier. We need to make a regular habit of talking about these heart issues, so the line of communication is always open. One of my friends shared that she often goes to her parents with her heart-struggles,

> "Now that I have made it a regular practice to go to my parents with my struggles, it has become easier to share these feelings. I have also become more burdened to talk with them about 'little things' as they arise. I just go to my mom or dad and say, 'Can I talk to you a minute about something?' They are always very willing to stop what they are doing and talk with me; more often than not, our conversation lasts longer than a few minutes—sometimes hours! No matter how nerve-wracking, embarrassing, and exposing it may be to unleash your private feelings, I encourage you to do it. It will be so worth it!"

Radiant Purity

Let us allow Christ to work a beautiful transformation in our life, as we surrender our heart and thoughts to Him in every area. As we pursue the everlasting beauty found in a life hid in Christ, He will make us true radiant gems of purity. Remember the admonition and promise found in Colossians 3:2-5:

> "Set your affection on things *above*, not on things on the earth.
> For ye are dead, and *your life is hid with Christ in God*.
> When Christ, who is our life, shall appear,
> THEN SHALL YE ALSO APPEAR WITH HIM IN GLORY."

on my shelf... RELATED RESOURCES

AUDIO:

– *The Ministry of Marriage* by Dr. Voddie Baucham (The Vision Forum Inc., 4719 Blanco Road, San Antonio, TX 76212; www.visionforum.com)

– *What Our Father Taught Us About Boys* by Anna Sofia & Elizabeth Botkin (Western Conservatory of Arts and Sciences; www.westernconservatory.org)

BOOKS:

– *Least Said, Soonest Mended* by Agnes Giberne (Keepers of the Faith, P.O. Box 100, Ironwood, MI 49938; www.keepersofthefaith.com)

– *Raising Maidens of Virtue* by Mrs. Stacy McDonald (Books on the Path, P.O. Box 436, Barker, TX 77413; www.booksonthepath.com)

– *Before You Meet Prince Charming* by Sarah Mally (Tomorrow's Forefathers, P.O. Box 11451, Cedar Rapids, IA, 52410; www.radiantpurity.com)

– *The Pursuit of Holiness* by Jerry Bridges (NavPress, P.O. Box 35001, Colorado Springs, CO, 80935; 800.366.7788)

a family daughter...
SHILOH A. STRANG

A YOUNG GIRL *clothed in strength and dignity softly walks down the path leading towards her humble home. Espying her father, she quickens her pace and runs to him, her golden hair tumbling down her shoulders. Clasped in his strong arms she looks up into his affectionate face. "I love you Daddy," she quietly whispers...*

This is a beautiful and lovely picture of femininity. Today, we live in a society where the picture of inward beauty—true femininity—is twisted and muddled. Our world tells young ladies that it is okay to be masculine, it is okay to compete against men. Sadly, many girls believe these lies. They throw away their God-given femininity in return for the World's garb. I would like to encourage you, as young ladies, to embrace your girlhood years and delight in your femininity.

In the Bible, Psalm 45:11-13a says: *"So shall the king greatly desire thy beauty: for he is they Lord; and worship thou him. The king's daughter is all glorious within."* Since we claim to be King's daughters, we must be all glorious within. One way we can do this is by being feminine. Here are some ways we can be feminine:

— **Dress like a lady:** Wearing pretty, lovely, modest, and feminine clothing will not only make you feel feminine, but other people will also treat you appropriately. Whenever my mother, sisters, and I go out, people comment on our dresses. Even if we are wearing our simple denim jumpers, people act as if we were dressed in silk. Because our society rarely sees ladies in modest apparel, it is pleasant and refreshing to see girls embodying femininity.

— **Act like a lady:** In your manners you should show yourself to be like the virtuous woman in Proverbs 31. In speaking, speak only in a way which will edify your hearers. Do not be obnoxious, crude, or selfish in your language. Instead bring forth gentleness, respectfulness, and humility in your speech. You can say something with meaning and yet speak gently.

— **Seek Encouragement:** Find other young ladies who also delight in their femininity, to benefit from their examples. For those of you who enjoy reading, books are a wonderful resource of encouragement as well. Some good books include *So Much More* by Anna Sofia and Elizabeth Botkin; *How to Be a Lady* by Harvey Newcomb; *Dear Princess* by Mary Landis; *Beautiful Girlhood* by M. Hale; or *Raising Maidens of Virtue* by Stacy McDonald.

— **Above All Else:** The Bible brings the best encouragement for a young lady. Some verses on the subject of daughters are Psalm 45, Psalm 144, Proverbs 31, Titus 2, and the marvelous books of Ruth and Esther. Be like the Bereans and search the Scriptures daily (Acts 17:11). You will be amazed at how much encouragement you will draw from the Word of God.

— **Last of All:** Be polished as it says in Psalm 144:12b: *"That your daughters may be as cornerstones polished after* the similitude of a palace." In your dress, manner, speech, and character—be polished. If your family was about to step into a beautifully furnished palace you would most likely check yourself. "Am I dressed fittingly to meet royalty? Are my actions and speech refined?" Apply this to your life. Remember you are a King's daughter, who must be all glorious within. The Lord Jesus is far more royal than any celebrity you will ever meet; after all He is the King of kings. In anything and everything you do, beautify yourself for Him.

I encourage you to not only delight in your femininity, but to also embrace your blessed daughterhood, and perhaps someday noble womanhood. Rise up, oh daughters of Zion! Hold tight to your calling and delight in your femininity.

SHILOH STRANG (17) lives in rural Boring, Oregon with her family of seven—plus 126 farm animals! Shiloh enjoys music, sewing, reading, writing, and crocheting, and anything to do with babies. She would like to be a wife, a mother, and a midwife someday.

"Do you love gaudy dresses
and useless ornaments, YOUNG READER?
Learn to understand the real beauty of simplicity.
With a taste refined by the study of nature,
and a mind absorbed by nobler things,
you will despise the vain ornaments that silly girls love."[8]

—CHRISTOPH VON SCHMID

"Walk in wisdom toward them that are without, redeeming the time."

[COLOSSIANS 4:5]

"Lord, make me to know mine end, & the measure of my days, what it is; that I may know how frail I am."

[PSALM 39:4]

CHAPTER EIGHT

The APPOINTED TIME

MY BROTHER, NATHAN, is our faithful goat milker. Rain, snow, sleet, or shine, he diligently milks every morning and evening without complaint. One day, my dad decided to give Nathan a day off from his farm chores. Later, Dad made an interesting observation—instead of sleeping in or playing while we did his chores, Nathan came outside and helped us. When I asked myself what I would have done if I had the day off, I had to admit that I would have taken advantage of the extra time by doing something more enjoyable. I realized how right Dad was about Nathan's selflessness!

Life is not about ourselves. How did Jesus spend His time on earth? Was He pleasing Himself, or was He serving His Father? Jesus, Ruler of all the earth, obeyed His authority completely. Who are we to do otherwise? It is good to evaluate the way we spend our time with the example of the Lord Jesus. Do we do only what we are required in household chores and then do our own thing? Do the things we involve ourselves in bring momentary pleasure or do we seek to glorify God?

Kept for the Master's Use is a very thought-provoking and encouraging read. It has challenged me to commit our every moment, thought, and movement to the Lord Jesus Christ. We must choose who we will serve and glorify with our time.

> "If we have gone so far as to say 'Take my moments,' have we gone the step further, and really let Him take them—really entrusted them to Him? It is no good to say 'take' when we do not let go... So let us with full trust in His power, first commit those slippery moments to Him—put them right in His hand—and then we may trustfully and happily say, 'Lord keep them for me!'"[1]

We should surrender our plans daily to the Lord: He is completely able to handle our time. His way is always better, even if different from what we planned. We may not feel like we did "all we needed to do," but when we do His will, we will accomplish all that He deems necessary. We must then obey His leading for our time; these prompts may come in the form of interruptions from little brother or questions from a sister, but even these things we must cheerfully accept for Christ's sake.

I have experienced the joys of giving my day to the Lord. On one particular day, I determined to use all extra time I had to serve my family. I do not recall what I actually did that day; it seemed insignificant to me at the time—but at the end of the day, Mom commented on all I had done. God had obviously used my day for His glory because I had surrendered it to His will, though I may not have necessarily planned what He did. The Lord's definition of a "successful" day may be different from ours, but we should keep our eyes focused on eternity—what will make a true difference?

The Lord has shown me that many times I work on projects I enjoy rather than developing useful homemaking skills. I do not always prefer to cook or clean, but I must place my *desires* aside and use my days to benefit my current and future family, because this is what God has called me to do.

CHAPTER EIGHT — *The Appointed Time*

Content Home Helpers

The productivity of our lives will be largely determined by where our focus lies—whether on serving others or pleasing ourselves. The *key* to living a fruitful life in the home is not focusing on self, but instead seeking to bring glory to our Lord. I want to encourage you to open your eyes to the needs around you and use your abilities for Christ, whatever those tasks may be. This season that we have as girls, while we are free from the responsibilities of keeping our own home, is a wide-open opportunity to serve others.

When we are alert for tasks that we can help with and people we can bless, what an incredible tool we can be in God's Kingdom! When I opened my eyes to the needs around me, I have noticed many areas that were vying for my attention and time. Often, my parents do not have time to work on various projects around our home because they have other more pressing responsibilities; I have been able to undertake tasks like repainting rooms, refinishing wood floors, decorating our home with photography, helping to keep the home tidy and clean, or sewing clothing. Picking up small chores also helps Mom have more time to focus on more important tasks. For example, I can help keep the house clean by dusting and sweeping areas that are not normally top priority. Simply wiping down baseboards, cleaning dirt and fingerprints off the walls, or giving the floor a good sweeping makes "cleaning day" less tedious and keeps the home more presentable. If I wipe down a room or two each weekday, it only takes a few minutes and becomes a habit. The things you can help your family with will be different, but purpose to look around and help where needed.

Being willing to help with these things we can do in our homes will make such a blessed difference. Do not overlook these "small" areas while searching for something that seems "more important." It can be easy for daughters to become discouraged because they feel they are not accomplishing anything worthwhile; "all they do" is help with household duties. Last year, the Lord taught me an important lesson. I felt like I was not really doing anything, just watching days pass while doing "mundane" tasks around the home. Unknowingly, I had adopted the world's career-mindset that I needed to do something bigger to be useful. I groped along, trying to think of something "important" I could do. Then, the Lord showed me that the "little" daily tasks are really what He wants me to be content in doing with *joy*! It is not necessarily some big project, career, ministry, or skill that matters in His sight. He wants me to be content in doing whatever He places in front of me. Sister, if the Lord has you at home "only" serving your family by helping your mom cook, clean, and care for your siblings, you are doing the most important thing—do not think you need to do something "bigger."

Scheduling

We should evaluate what projects need to be accomplished, planning our days so that none are wasted. We also need to regularly ask our parents if they have projects we can do that would be helpful, and incorporate these tasks into our schedule. Disciplining ourselves to follow a schedule will help us remain focused; but more importantly, it will help us use the time God has given us wisely. If we make scheduled life a habit now, we will find it very beneficial later as homemakers. A married friend shared with me how thankful she is that she learned to live by a schedule when she was younger, because now as a mother, with more things that must be done each day, she can more easily stay on task and complete these chores.

Spare Moments

I once read this challenging quote, "Today you should not only be older, but also wiser, closer to God, stronger in character, and more capable to do His work than ever before" (author unknown). I have to ask myself if this is true of my life. Do I capture every minute that God grants me? Time passes whether we are glorifying God or not, whether we want it to pass or not. It is our responsibility to use it wisely.

Every fleeting second in our day is very important; one minute wasted may not sound significant, but it can never be recovered. Each of these minutes adds up when you start multiplying—ten minutes every day for a year totals sixty hours, or three full days. What a great amount of good can be done in three days if used wisely! We need to embrace every single minute that is before us for the glory of God.

Oftentimes, I have a few spare minutes during the day while waiting for someone or en route in the van. I cannot afford to waste these minutes "just waiting." Realizing the important of these opportunities, I was prompted to make a list of things I can do during extra moments. This is displayed in a prominent place so I can refer to it easily when I have extra time between tasks:

- Do a quick clean-up run through the house—put toys away, align shoes, sweep the floor, wash any dirty dishes, do the laundry, or any miscellaneous tasks that need to be done.
- See if my parents need help or be available to talk to them.
- Spend time with a sibling, helping them with a chore or just chatting with them.
- Pray for my parents and siblings, especially if they are having a hard time at the moment. Ask for peace, wisdom, joyfulness, strength, and patience in their lives.
- Pray for people on my prayer list, for our nation, for a closer walk with Jesus—whoever He brings to mind at the moment.
- Write a Scripture verse on a postcard with a note of encouragement for someone on my prayer list to let them know I am praying for them that day.
- Write a note of encouragement to a family member.

We can also use these spare moments to seek the Lord. Just fifteen minutes each day amounts to about five days per year. If we went to Jesus during every in-between time of the day, I am sure we can find at least this much time daily to commune with Him. How can we do this during the spare moments of our day? Some thoughts are,

- Pray that God would reveal sins in your life that are hidden from your sight, and strength to overcome them.
- Read a passage in the Bible. You might find it helpful to look up the passage in a commentary or concordance to gain a fuller understanding of the context.
- Work on Scripture memory or mentally review verses already memorized.
- Sing to the Lord.
- Write in your journal what the Lord has recently done in your life, so you will be able to look back and praise Him.

These are just some things we can do in the little "in-between" moments of life; more time should be allocated for each of these areas regularly. I suggest that you make a list of things that *you* can do in your spare minutes. It all boils down to using every *moment* for His glory.

Today is the Hour

It once seemed to me that my "teenage" years would last forever, but I am finding how fleeting these years truly are! I know that my character and habits are more firmly formed the older I grow, and it sobers me to think that what I am today is largely who I will be the rest of my life. With this realization, God has impressed upon me that I need to make the most of each fleeting day. Am I allowing His conviction in my heart today or am I putting it off for a "more convenient" day? When I wake up each morning, do I see in my mind's eye only a list of tasks I need to accomplish, only deadlines that need to be met? Or, do I feel the Spirit

CHAPTER EIGHT — *The Appointed Time*

prompting me to focus on an area in my life that needs refining? Am I rejoicing for another day to be with my family and worship the Lord?

The Lord has also shown me that I am often side-tracked with other goals. I never thought I spent much time "day dreaming," but God has shown me that I spend far too much time thinking of "how good the future will be," forgetting that *today* is the opportunity to actually work toward that. Time is too valuable to dream away, and we will be sorely disappointed when the time comes if we have developed expectations that are too high.

For this reason, I have made a three-year commitment to focus on specific areas that need growth in my life. In these months and years, I desire to focus on the Lord alone, to trust Him to work out my future while I am focused on Him, not worrying about it. I cannot do anything good of my own accord,[2] so I am giving my life to Him with no reservations. I realize that this will not be easy, and there will be fiery trials to face, some of which I have already experienced. But the work He can do in my life is far more valuable than the sacrifice it requires. Will you commit yourself to Him so He can mold you into His image? Will you choose to focus on Him and allow His work in your life? You might want to ask your parents to keep you accountable in your commitment.

I like to make goals in my journal for each new year. It helps me look back and see what the Lord has done in my life. The past few years I have made very specific goals which helps me keep focused. Here are some examples, but let God point out areas in *your* life which need growth.

— Be open to the needs of my family and areas to serve them
— Seek ways to lighten Mom's load and duties in the home
— Pray for my family members by name each day

Similarly, my friend Jenny Florio challenges,

"I would encourage you to take time to develop a purpose-statement for your life. What gifts and passions has God given to you, and how will you use them for His glory? What chapters and books of Scripture would you like to memorize? How exactly will you serve your family and community? Writing these goals down on paper has greatly encouraged me to run the race without becoming distracted."

Focus on...

At times it is easy to think about or list character traits that I desire in a future husband. When I begin to do this, the Lord reminds me that what I desire in a mate is what *I* must become myself. I have heard the profound statement, "You must become yourself what you want your mate to be." How true this is! It is not fair to ask God for a man who loves the Lord with all of his being, if I am not willing to do that *myself*. It is so much more important that I work in my own life than dream about a husband. Also, we will attract who we are—if we are disrespectful to our parents, then a man who honors his parents will certainly not find us attractive!

Most girls tend to have this fairy-tell vision of marriage. Sister, do not fool yourself; do not make expectations that can never be fulfilled by a husband—if you do, you will experience disappointment, and possibly damage your future marriage. Your future husband will not be able to fulfill all of your emotional needs; he will be human just as you are. One happily married friend advised me,

> "There definitely are areas to give up when the Lord brings 'prince charming' into one's life. That is why it is not advantageous to have a huge list of what one wants in a husband. It is better to focus on Jesus, and be delighted at His perfect choice. Your future husband will not be perfect, but he will be the one God has ordained as a sanctification tool in your life."

Instead of thinking of all the things we want our future husband to be, why don't we make a list of areas *we* ourselves must grow in to become a godly woman of God? Since I think it is safe to say that none of us have reached a state where we do not need further spiritual growth, let us examine our lives according to God's Word.³ Here is a brief list of qualities the Bible gives of the godly woman; I encourage you to honestly evaluate your life, *Is this true of my life?*

- Do I truly fear the Lord? (Proverbs 31:30)
- Am I sober in actions; self-controlled in the way I voice my opinions and feelings? (Titus 2:4)
- Am I discreet—quiet and modest in spirit and dress? (Titus 2:5)
- Am I chaste—clean, pure, and modest in my attitude? (Titus 2:5, I Peter 3:3-4)
- Do I honor my authorities in *all things*—actions, words, attitude? (Titus 2:4) Am I always immediately obedient, submissive to authority? Do I follow leadership willingly?
- Do I resist instruction? (Titus 2:5)
- Do I display a quarrelsome attitude? (Proverbs 19:13, 21:9)
- Do I love children; am I always patient with them? (Titus 2:4)
- Do I have a shamefaced attitude before men? (I Timothy 2:9)
- Do I have an instructing attitude toward men? Do I ever correct or instruct my father or other men? (I Corinthians 14:34)
- Do I work hard and diligently; am I willing to help my family in areas they can use my support and help? (Proverbs 31:15)

It can be hard to answer these honestly; ask your parents to help you evaluate your life according to Scripture and share their thoughts. When I look at my life beside the bright light and high standard of the Bible, I become uncomfortable and convicted of many areas that need growth. On the other hand, if I compare myself to others, I do not feel that conviction. *"He is like unto a man beholding his natural face in a glass.... But whoso looketh into the perfect law of liberty...this man shall be blessed in his deed"* (James 1:23-25). It is important that we keep the Word as our standard.

The Appointed Time

Now is the time, Sister, to *"seek ye the LORD while he may be found"* (Isaiah 55:6). Do not wait—*"for what is your life? It is even a vapor"* (James 4:14). If the Lord wills, in just a few years we may be wives and mothers. Do not think, *When I get married, I'll have all the time in the world to invest in my relationship with God.* One godly friend shared with me, after she married and had several young children, how true she has found I Corinthians 7:34 to be. She testified that it is difficult to study God's Word as much as she could as a daughter, because now she has to fill the responsibilities of being a keeper of her home. Truly, unmarried women have time to "care for the things of the Lord." Let us treasure this, and embrace every moment for the glory of God.

---

on my shelf...
RELATED RESOURCES

AUDIO:

- *Jennie B. and the Pilot* by Mrs. Jennie Chancey (The Vision Forum Inc., 4719 Blanco Road, San Antonio, TX 76212; www.visionforum.com)

- *Strength & Dignity for Daughters* by Anna Sofia & Elizabeth Botkin (The Vision Forum Inc., 4719 Blanco Road, San Antonio, TX 76212; www.visionforum.com)

BOOKS:

- *Jeff McLean: His Courtship* by Mr. & Mrs. Stephen Castleberry (Castleberry Press, P.O. Box 337, Poplar, WI 54864) *This book lays out biblical character traits a godly woman should have, and has encouraged me to evaluate my own life and goals.* —SLB

- *Passionate Houswives Desperate For God* by Mrs. Jennie Chancey and Mrs. Stacy McDonald (The Vision Forum Inc.; 800.440.0022)

a family daughter...
HANNAH SCHOENFELDER

THE LORD HAS recently opened my eyes to how I have not been spending my unmarried days for His glory. I would love to share what He has been teaching me and encourage you to avoid the same mistakes, as a daughter at home.

I have dreamed of marrying, having a family, and caring for a home of my own, since I was very young; I especially dreamed of marrying young (about age 18) so I could have as many children as possible. I still carry those dreams, but the Lord has taught me to trust in His will, not my own.

Upon graduating from high school in our homeschool, not much changed. Instead of school, I filled my time with projects that I had not had time for before. I began dreaming of books to write, made things for my hope chest, read books, and began a book of ideas for my own future home. I did my chores and helped when needed, but my days were mainly scheduled with my own projects—scrap-booking, sewing, computer work, writing, drawing, or cleaning my room.

As I grew older, there were more opportunities for ministry outside of the home. Since my sister and I did not have jobs and were at home most of the time, we could do all the things no one else had time to do. We were called on to baby sit, direct Vacation Bible School and Christmas programs, do garden work, clean, decorate, make wedding cakes, and lead a Bright Lights discipleship group.

All these things are good and I wholeheartedly agree that young ladies should do these kind of things. It all needs to be in balance and in accordance with God's design, though. As we look at Scripture, many of the young ladies were found serving in their father's households, not out and about ministering and working, as in the account of Rebekah. The lesson I have been learning is my home and family comes first. This is where God has placed me and where I can serve Him best and prepare for the future.

When I began to realize I was not serving my family properly, I saw that there were so many areas in our home that were falling apart because I only had time for the minimum required work, before I hurried off to my own projects. As I began to do things such as straightening, picking up, and scrubbing the home, and put homemaking and serving my family above my own projects, our home changed and areas that had been falling apart improved. I also realized that if I cannot be responsible to care for my home now when I have a mom and two sisters helping, I can not possibly expect to be able to care for my own home efficiently in the future.

It can be more "fun" and look more glamorous to be involved in ministries outside of the home, have a job, or travel. God may open those doors for us, but our main calling is to be at home serving our fathers, helping our mothers, caring for our siblings, and learning to be a keeper at home. That is the highest work and will be worth a lot to your "prince charming" someday, if that is in the Lord's will for you.

For me, some of the things I had enjoyed doing before had to go because they were hindering my family or taking up too much of my time. I am still involved in a lot of ministries, but all of them are ministries I have found that I can do without sacrificing time from my family, or it is a ministry our family has decided to do together. God has given us daughters a great opportunity, and we can be an outstanding blessing to our families. Your home should be kept more clean, tidy and well-ordered because of your attention; your parents should be more free to care for your younger siblings; you should be capable and willing to take on more responsibilities for your parents; your siblings should thrive under your example, attention, and time spent with them. Just imagine a young lady who is ready and willing to serve her family where needed, who drops her own work to help her family. What a way to honor our parents!

I hope these things will encourage you. I know I need to hear this over and over, because the world, and even well-meaning Christians, pressure young ladies to get out from under their parents' authority, "get a life" and their own independence. I am always learning and have not achieved any of these things to the fullest. Everyday, however, I can make choices in the little things and with the Lord's strength, I can return to my home and the place God wants me to be.

HANNAH SCHOENFELDER, 22, is a homeschool graduate from Bemidji, Minnesota, where she lives with her family of seven on a hobby farm. She enjoys organizing, writing, crocheting, and cooking, among other homemaking skills. She continues to learn everyday from the Lord and delights in spending time with Him. She and her sister publish a little magazine and enjoy encouraging and challenging other young ladies towards biblical womanhood in that way.

"If thou *doest not speak* to warn the wicked from his way,
that wicked man shall die in his iniquity;
but his blood will I *require* at thine hand.
Nevertheless, if thou *warn* the wicked of his way to turn from it;
if he do not turn from his way, he shall die in his iniquity;
but thou hast *delivered* thy soul.
Therefore, O thou son of man, speak unto the house of Israel...
As I live, saith the Lord God, I HAVE NO PLEASURE
in the death of the wicked;
but that the wicked *turn* from his way and *live*:
turn ye, turn ye from your evil ways;
for WHY WILL YE DIE, O house of Israel?"

[EZEKIEL 33:8-11]

"I am the light of the world:
he that followeth me shall *not* walk in darkness,
but shall have the **light of life.**"

[JOHN 8:12]

CHAPTER NINE

Reflecting the Light

HAVE YOU EVER thought about the contact you had with a clerk at the store, or the salesperson you talked to on the phone, or the young mother who was shopping at the grocery store when you were? Out of millions of people, God gave *you* this brief contact. These are not chance happenings; God ordains these meetings. The thought amazes me!

Recently, I had to make a call to register some computer software, and while waiting for the verification number, the operator filled the time asking questions. This eventually led our conversation to the topic of our location. When he said that he was in India, I curiously asked, "What religion are you?" He proudly answered, "I'm Hindu." I was amazed; I was actually speaking to a person who was of a religion I had often heard about, but not realized how alive and real it was. I thought, *What is the coincidence of me talking to this person on the other side of the world—a Hindu?! And of all times, while I am sitting here at my own desk at home!* That seemed extraordinary "chance" indeed, but it was actually a providential appointment by the Lord, Who knows this person and his future—what a great opportunity this was to share the Gospel.

Though Jesus gave His life to save mankind, all transgress against Him, and the vast majority reject Him.[1] Romans 3:23 reminds us that *all* are sinners; we all have transgressed against God, and we all fall short of His perfect standard. For this, God demands punishment: *"The Lord Jesus shall be revealed from heaven with his mighty angels, in flaming fire taking vengeance on them that know not God, and that obey not the gospel of our Lord Jesus Christ: who shall be punished with everlasting destruction from the presence of the Lord"* (II Thessalonians 1:7-9).[2] Yet, God is merciful, and the story does not end there. Titus 2:11 beautifully proclaims, *"The grace of God that bringeth salvation hath appeared to all men."* He provided a way that we may still enjoy His presence in Heaven for eternity, if we accept the sacrifice that was given on behalf of our sins—His perfect Son, Jesus Christ. Those who *"call upon the name of the Lord shall be saved"* (Romans 10:13). To be saved, we as sinners must confess our sin against God, and accept Jesus as our personal Savior. When we embrace Jesus as our Savior, we are *"made free from sin, and become servants to God, ye have your fruit unto holiness, and the end everlasting life"* (Romans 6:22). The Lord will continue the sanctification process in His children's lives and transform us more into His likeness.

As Christ's servants saved by His grace, we must live as a beacon of this salvation—reflect the light of Christ's presence in our hearts. We must share this wonderful news with the Lost who are bound toward an eternity without the Lord Jesus. No matter how good someone may seem to be, we must remember that whoever does not accept salvation in Christ (Romans 10:9), will spend eternity estranged from His presence. We must not lose sight of this, getting side-tracked by other things. Many times I become so focused on my agenda that I do not notice the hurting people around me; I forget that I can point them to Jesus, Who can save them from an endless, dreadful torment. He is not

CHAPTER NINE — *Reflecting The Light*

willing that *any* perish—*"but that all should come to repentance"* (II Peter 3:9). Christ says, *"This is the will of Him that sent me, that every one which seeth the Son, and believeth on Him, may have everlasting life: and I will raise him up at the last day"* (John 6:40).

The Lord gives us so many chances to witness for Him; in fact, everyone we come in contact with should see the light of Christ in our life. We should be zealous to share the Gospel with every person in our path, because God guides the very steps of our feet and knows who we will meet. My mom adds wisdom on the witnessing opportunities that surround all believers,

WHILE LIVING IN KOREA several years ago, the Lord taught me the invaluable lesson of His supplying people to witness to as He sees the need—not as I feel the need.

"I am still not sure how anyone could feel lonely amidst a city of 23 million people, but I did. At the time, we had five young children, we were homeschooling, and we did not go out in the city often. Yet, when we did, the Lord showed us favor. The Korean people love children and were immediately attracted to our small children. They would say, 'You are rich!' We were, but not in the physical sense in which they were speaking; we were richly blessed by God.

"The Lord showed me that He would provide others to witness to, without me even having to seek them out. One day, as two Koreans were in our home making repairs, I realized the Lord constantly sent people to our door. We had various workmen, neighbors, music teachers, and acquaintances that visited almost daily for the three years we lived there! It was an exciting time and a well-learned lesson. So, when I start to complain about the lack of fellowship or lack of opportunities to be a witness for the Lord, I remember that He sends people when He knows best. The Lord continues to bring people to our door everyday via our home business. I have ample contact with outsiders everyday."

See, opportunities arise for us to witness all the time. As Christ's servants, every part of our life must be transformed by His presence in our heart. Romans 12:2 commands believers to *"be not conformed to this world: but be ye transformed by the renewing of your mind."* When this is true of us, the Lord can use our very life to shine brightly for His sake. These areas include...

Our Speech

"That I may...tell of all thy wondrous works." (Psalm 26:7)

What we say can turn others away or point the Lost to Christ. When we are joyful in the Lord's salvation, we will want to share it with others. Do our words direct others to the Lord of our salvation? Showing we care by listening to others' burdens is one way we should demonstrate Jesus' love. People need someone who will listen, and this is an opportunity to share the One who cares about their needs. We need to develop a genuine concern and ultimate love for others as Jesus had, for *"when we were enemies, we were reconciled to God by the death of his Son"* (Romans 5:10). We need to be ready to share the Gospel with others at any time.

Our Actions

"Ye should show forth the praises of him who hath called you out of darkness into his marvelous light." (I Peter 2:9)

Our actions are a witness, whether in a good or a bad light. Our actions potentially have more influence than tracts we may hand out or anything we "preach"—because others can see the *difference* that Jesus makes in our life. Can others see the joy of the Lord in my face, or do they think that *I* am the one who is "missing out"? It is my prayer that those I come in contact with see Something they need, Something they cannot obtain through new styles, friends, or money—Jesus.

Our Joy

"I will rejoice in the LORD, I will joy in the God of my salvation." (Habakkuk 3:18)

I remember watching a group of school children gather for a picture one day. One grumpy girl announced quite loudly, "I have already smiled once today. I don't want to smile again!" While this might have seemed humorous, I realized how true this attitude is of many, how few add a smile to their face. Smiles which radiate the serene joy of Christ are such a beautiful blessing. As Christians, don't we have a huge reason to be joyful? Jesus has saved and loved us!

> "*The love of Christ* is not an absorbing, but a radiating love. The more we love Him, the more we shall most certainly love others."[3]
> —Francis Havergal (1879)

Our joyful attitude will be a great witness to others; this simple thing is so noticeable in a hurting world. See how many times you can smile in one day; remember the Reason you have to be joyful. This certainly is an area in which I need to grow!

Our Appearance

"But ye are a chosen generation, a royal priesthood, a holy nation, a peculiar people." (I Peter 2:9)

As Christ's ambassadors, we are called to be a peculiar people so we can *"show forth the praises of Him."* We should not be conformed to the world but reserved for the Lord; we *"are the salt of the earth: but if the salt have lost his savor, wherewith shall it be salted? it is thenceforth good for nothing"* (Matthew 5:13). "Salt" assumes that we have a distinct and different "taste"; "light" assumes we are distinguished, as a beacon on a hill. If we do not have distinctness from the world, we cannot shine as a light. When we conform to the world's fashions, we show our admiration for it. Yet do we want to honor the world in its sin? *"We are of God, and the whole world lieth in wickedness"* (I John 5:19). We are not part of the world if we are Christ's children, and should not seek to imitate it. *"I will punish the world for their evil, and the wicked for their iniquity"* (Isaiah 13:11). A Christ-honoring appearance, untainted from ungodly influences, is a strong witnessing tool.

Our Attitude

"For what is our hope, or joy, or crown of rejoicing? Are not even ye in the presence of our Lord Jesus Christ at his coming?" (I Thessalonians 2:19)

We should not be self-conscious of our testimony for Christ, neither should we have a self-righteous attitude. Be careful not to judge others, especially by something you know about them or the way they look. Judging is not our job: *"He that speaketh evil of his brother, and judgeth his brother, speaketh evil of the law, and judgeth the law"* (James 4:11). I have found myself unconsciously judging others before I even know them; often I later realize my early accusations were inaccurate and sinful. I have repented of this sin and pray that I do not display an attitude which hinders the witness I can be for His sake. Once our family had contact with a woman who held an unbiblical occupation. Because I did not agree with her, I didn't make an effort to witness to her. Then the Lord convicted me that instead of turning from her, I should *especially* make an effort to be kind to her; maybe He would open doors for us to be a blessing in her life. Soon after I was convicted of my attitude, I had the opportunity to talk with her. A few weeks later we met this lady's adult daughter; I was shocked when she came to me and said, "My mom always talks about your family after she sees you, so I thought I'd come to meet you!" What a slap in my face—as I realized her mother was sruggling spiritually. Consequently, we had the opportunity to know both the mother and the daughter better, which has been a blessing.

Our Heart

> "A good man out of the good treasure of his heart bringeth forth that which is good; and an evil man out of the evil treasure of his heart bringeth forth that which is evil: for of the abundance of the heart his mouth speaketh." (Luke 6:45)

Our actions are only an outward manifestation of the state of our heart. If we do not deeply, truly love the Lord, our attempts to be a good witness for Him are vain. We cannot be an effective witness if our heart is not in the right place. Just "checking off the marks"—actions, speech, appearance, fill-the-blank—will not make us a bright light for Christ. The starting place is loving the Lord, desiring His will, and living as God desires of us as daughters—honoring our parents and His Blueprint for our life. When we simply do this, when we apply ourselves duteously to the everyday "mundane" tasks in our father's home, then our lives will be a strong testimony and a light for Him. Are you content in honoring the Lord through serving your family right now, or are you just at home "until you turn eighteen"? Your submissive and loving attitude will be communicated through your life choices, and shine brightly to the Lost. Going across the world to "be a missionary" is hardly the only way to witness. It starts in the home in the small areas (Matthew 25:23). My friend Grace Pennington (19) encourages girls to turn their heart to their home, where the Lord has great ministry opportunities awaiting them,

> "One verse that came to my attention lately was from I Samuel, 'To obey is better than sacrifice' (15:22). So many girls want to go out

onto the mission field away from their families, and make all these 'sacrifices' so they can serve God the way they think they should, when He has told us in His Word what He wants us to do; and He would rather we obey His revealed will for us as daughters in our fathers' homes, than if we run off and do our own 'sacrificial' thing."

Our Focus

"Looking unto Jesus the author and finisher of our faith; who for the joy that was set before him endured the cross, despising the shame, and is set down at the right hand of the throne of God." (Hebrews 12:2)

What we dwell on and the attitude we harbor largely determines how we will shine for Jesus Christ. When I am thinking self-centered thoughts, how can I shine for my Master? How can I act in a way that seeks to bring glory to Someone other than myself?

In particular, the Lord has shown me what I should be focusing on when I prepare to go somewhere. What are my thoughts when I get dressed to go out? Am I thinking about *myself*—what to wear? Or am I preparing for the opportunities that I may have to witness for Jesus wherever we go?

When I keep my mind on the Lord Jesus and the needs of others, my reactions are not self-centered. When someone turns and stares at our family, the thoughts that come to mind are not self-conscious, like *Here we go! They think we are so weird...I know I look like an alien to them!* Or, *They keep pointing at all my siblings!* Rather, when I am focusing on the Lord, instead of thinking how funny I feel compared to the half-dressed females in a checkout line beside me, I pray, "Lord Jesus, bless those ladies, and bring comfort to their hurting souls," Or, "Please help me display a gentle spirit for Your sake!" I have to remind myself that there are other people in the world besides myself! Sometimes I get so wrapped up in my own bubble that I lose sight of the eternal perspective. I am just one person among millions—yet called to be a servant of Christ. Let us keep this perspective in mind. When you are preparing for someone's arrival, for a trip, or for errand day, prepare your heart to witness by focusing on Jesus. You will be amazed at how much more He can use you when you are not focusing on yourself.

Our Influence

Several years ago, I met two godly older sisters who befriended me and took time out of their busy life to mentor me. Every Sunday, one of these sweet sisters would make a point to call me—even if it was only for a few minutes on their way to church. They openly shared their spiritual struggles and how the Lord was working in their hearts. They also would ask what the Lord was doing in my life or what I was learning in my Bible reading, and this accountability was an incredible blessing for my spiritual growth. I would always get off the phone so encouraged.

When our family was going through a difficult trial that year, I knew I could call my friends at any time and they would listen. Throughout that time I struggled in many areas, but they could offer encouragement, having gone through similar situations themselves when they were younger. Having an older girl to listen and offer wisdom was such an encouragement in my walk with the Lord.

I am sure these girls never befriended me because it was fun for *them*. I am nearly a decade younger, and they certainly could have found many other girls who they personally would have benefited more from. In our peer-dependent society, we often seek out friends who are our peers with similar interests. This is fine—as long as we do not get so wrapped up in these friendships that we never think twice about others who may be lonely, or need godly encouragement or an example.[4]

These young ladies blessed me by just being there and caring about my life. Because they did not allow the vast difference in our ages to hinder our relationship, they gave me a visual goal of how a Christian daughter and sister lives when she is fully committed to her Savior. At a time in my life when I had few godly examples of daughters and was approaching the critical time of my teenage years, their lives gave me a vision of what I could strive to become. These girls never tried to seem perfect; rather, their humility and sincerity offered hope to me in my own struggles. They mentored me by simply sharing a glimpse into their heart. They deeply desired to please their Lord, and were grieved when they dishonored Him. As I was talking with one of the sisters one day, she shared that earlier in the week she had displayed a bad attitude. She was *weeping* as she related this to me, because it caused her great sorrow that she displeased her Savior. She so earnestly desired to please Him.

These friends continue to be godly examples for me, by choosing the path sparsely traveled, following the Lord's will now as mothers. I am so grateful to the Lord for their lives of obedience. The beautiful mentoring relationship these young ladies had in my life is an incredible fulfillment of God's design for older women to be a mature example to the younger. Titus 2:4-5 commands, *"That [the aged women] may teach the young women to be sober, love their husbands, to love their children, to be discreet, chaste, keepers at home, good, obedient to their own husbands."*

In the same way these young ladies greatly impacted my life, so do we each affect those who are younger. And our sphere of influence is not hindered by distance—these sisters were a continent away from me physically, yet their influence in my life was phenomenal. There are *always* younger girls who closely watch to see the way we handle life, even those we do not know about. They know more about us than we might think. I know from personal experience; I watch older Christian girls and study their lives. There are young ladies all over the globe whose lives of godliness I highly respect. Though I have personally met few of them, they still influence me through their writings, actions, dress, purity, and attitudes. Each, in her own way, is an example of what I want to become, by God's grace.

If, by observing one's life we glean so much, how much more influential a personal friendship is! When we do our part in encouraging those who are younger, we can have a positive impact in these lives for the glory of God. Watch for opportunities God may send your way to invest in a younger girl. Take time to talk with her or write her a note. You may never know what an impact your interest in her may have in her life! Share with her what God has been teaching you; do not "limit" your friendship because she is younger. We all were younger at one time! *Let no man despise thy youth; but be thou be an example of the believers*" (I Timothy 4:12). I cannot tell how many times I felt left out of an older girl's life, because she acted like, "You are just too young." No one wants to be looked down upon by someone they admire.

My little brother, Samuel, has shown me time and time again how true this concept is. Most of Samuel's "friends" are not his peers; usually they are three to four times his age. He constantly talks about and copies his "buddies," unhindered by the age gap. All they have done to win Samuel's admiration is to notice and befriend him. Joshua is Samuel's special "role model." Everything that Joshua does, Samuel imitates. Sometimes this gets scary—like when he tries to climb a tree upside down or fix the roof. Another friend showed an interest in Samuel, and has been a godly mentor as well. Young men who Samuel admires do not realize the impact they have on his life, yet they have a great influence on the kind of man my brother will someday become.

One night at a gathering of many large families, Samuel saw a young man who he really wanted to talk to and meet. I advised Samuel just to go up and say, "Hi!" So full of eager anticipation, Samuel, with a huge grin over his shoulder back to us, stood around where this guy was conversing with a friend. Imagine Samuel's disappointment, when this young man finished talking and walked right past Samuel's expectant face, paying him no attention. Undeterred, Samuel followed him around, but he simply did not notice my brother. Samuel was very disappointed when we left that night and he had not gotten to meet this young man whom he admired.

It is easy to overlook those who would treasure our friendship. When there are others present who may be lonely, we must make it a point to speak to them—or at least smile! I know it is so easy to spend time with those we most enjoy being around, but we should *never* leave others out. Have you ever been left out of a group because they were so self-engrossed they did not notice your presence—or worse, did see you but did not make any effort to include you? How did it make you feel? This has happened to me and I have felt unwanted, but at one gathering, a sweet young lady made a place for me to sit down and join their conversation. What a joy to listen to these godly young people exhort one another in the Lord. Beth blessed me greatly by inviting me to join them! Make an effort to show friendliness—whether or not you desire to talk with them or have similar interests. This especially is a blessing to those who are naturally shy.

We are influencing others every day, whether we want to or not, in a good or bad way. God has given this responsibility to each of us; it is not an option. *"Be thou an example of the believers"* (I Timothy 4:12). We should embrace it as an opportunity to shine for Him. Do not make excuses, *Oh, someone else can do it,* Or *I am not 'good enough'!* Are any of us truly good enough? Psalm 14:3 gives the resounding answer—*"They are all gone aside, they are all together become filthy: there is none that doeth good, no, not one."* By His grace, God can use us despite our faults. When we earnestly desire to please the Lord, even when we fail, we can be an example of repentance and perseverance.

CHAPTER NINE — *Reflecting The Light*

Acts of Thoughtfulness

My younger siblings, Mom, and I attended a monthly science class for homeschool families a few years ago, and most of the children in the class were under ten years old. The second month we attended class, I was having a rough day. As I stood in the shade of a tree watching the children eagerly catch butterflies, a little girl shyly walked up to me. She reached for my hand and said, "You look beautiful!"

Immediately my day was brightened by this girl who did not even know me, who was a fraction of my age. I smiled and replied, "Thank you!" She happily told me her name was Emma. At seven years of age, she was the oldest of four siblings. I can only imagine what a blessing her thoughtfulness is to her family and others around her. How often does a seven-year-old go out of her way to bless others? For that matter, how often does *anyone* joyfully reach out to everyone around?

During the rest of the class, little Emma tagged along beside me. She was so happy and full of life. I noticed that when the other children needed something, Emma considerately helped and encouraged them. Once another child made a guess about a chemical reaction. When his answer turned out to be correct, Emma exclaimed, "You're a genius!" I had to laugh. The next month as we arrived at class, I heard a joyful shout as Emma came running toward me, arms open to embrace me.

When we look around for ways to bless others we know—even if they are just acquaintances—what a light for Jesus we can be! The little acts of thoughtfulness can mean so much to someone—a happy smile, a kind word, a birthday card, bouquet of wild flowers, Scripture bookmark, just a hug—these seemingly "little" acts of thoughtfulness cost us little or nothing, but can go a long way in witnessing to others of Christ's love in our life. Let us ask Jesus to make us a more selfless image of Himself, looking for the needs of others, giving to others who are hurting.

The Will of Our Father

Ultimately, our witness for the Lord will be determined by our obedience to His will. Our Savior went about His Father's will—alone. *"For I came down from heaven, not to do mine own will, but the will of Him that sent me"* (John 6:38). He did not seek personal pleasure or desires. How much more should I, His redeemed child, seek God's will in every decision of life? In seemingly small daily choices I must ask, *What does God want me to do in this situation? How would Jesus best be represented right now?* Only through my complete obedience will my Father be glorified in my life, and only then will I reflect the light of Jesus to a hurting world—to a people in desperate need of Him.

We are influencing those whom we come in contact with for His eternal Kingdom. Are you using these opportunities for Christ? It *will* leave a mark in eternity.

RELATED RESOURCES

DVD:

– *The Culture Wars: Nothing is Neutral and Not All Gods are Alike* by Dr. Voddie Baucham (The Vision Forum Inc.; 800.440.0022)

Books:

– *If I Perish* by Esther Ahn Kim (Moody Publishers, 820 N. LaSalle Boulevard, Chicago, IL 60610; www.moodypublishing.com)

– *Mary Jones and Her Bible* reprinted by Lamplighter Publishing (P.O. Box 777, Waverly, PA 18471, 888.246.7735; www.lamplighter.net)

– *The Family* by J.R. Miller (The Vision Forum Inc.; 800.440.0022)

CHAPTER NINE — Reflecting The Light

— *Awaiting the Dawn* by Dorcas Hoover (Christian Light Publications, Harrisonburg, VA, 22802)

— *Evidence Not Seen* by Mrs. Darlene Deibler Rose (HarborCollins Publishers, 10 East 53rd Street, New York, NY 10022)

— *Mercy At Midnight* by Lois Hoadley Dick (Moody Publishers, 820 N. LaSalle Boulevard, Chicago, IL 60610; www.moodypublishing.com) *My friend and writing inspiration, Mrs. Dick, wrote this book.* —SLB

— *Through Gates of Splendor* by Elisabeth Elliot (Tyndale House Publishers, Wheaton, IL)

— *Amy Carmichael of Dohnavur* by Frank L. Houghton (Christian Literature Crusade; Box 1449, Fort Washington, PA 19034)

"Let this mind be in you, which was
also in Christ Jesus:
Who, being in the form of God,
thought it not robbery to be equal with God:

"But made himself of no reputation,
& took upon him the form of a servant,
and was made in the likeness of men:

"And being found in fashion as a man,
he humbled himself,
and became obedient unto *death*,
even the death of the cross.

"Wherefore God also hath highly exalted him,
and given him a name which is above every name:
That *at the name of Jesus every knee should bow,*
of things in heaven, & things in earth,
and things under the earth."

—PHILIPPIANS 2:5-10

a family daughter...
KARISSA HIEBERT

When considering this topic of being a witness, I had to think, first of all, why we desire to display Christ through our lives and proclaim His name.

— We have been Redeemed by the precious blood of Jesus Christ. "In my place, condemned He stood, sealed my pardon with His blood—hallelujah! what a Savior!" We have been bought with a price; how can we not give Him our all after He gave Himself so freely for us? How could we but desire that others find our Lord also, and the peace, joy, and purpose He gives? "Love so amazing, so divine, demands my soul, my life, my all!"

— We are Here for the Glory of God! Not for ourselves, our own pleasure, our own gain, or our own glory, but for Him alone. We are here to proclaim His name and further His glorious Kingdom! *"This people have I formed for Myself; they shall show forth My praise"* (Isaiah 43:21).

— He is Worthy! He is utterly worthy of all our heart's devotion. He is worthy of all honor from our lives, and worthy to be made known to all people (Revelation 4:11, 5:12).

Let us proclaim Him through our lives. *"Ye are the light of the world,"* Jesus said in Matthew 5:14. How can we, as young ladies, be salt and light in the world?

— Our Appearance: Modest, feminine dress is such a testimony. The World notices the difference, and often will comment on how refreshing it is. Do not be different for the sake of being different, but take delight in dressing like a princess of your heavenly King, and when someone comments on how you dress, direct it to Him for His glory. Be a witness through your outward appearance!

— Our Actions: There is much truth to the age-old quote, "Actions speak louder than words." If we say something, but do not live it out, or if our actions contradict what we say, we will not be an effective witness. The World is observing our lives, and godly actions speak volumes. They notice how we treat others, what we do, and what values are lived out through our lives.

— Our Speech: In today's world of lazy, slang, and unprofitable speech, it is a testimony to those around us when we speak properly, clearly, and profitably. A gentle, kind, joyful, and confident, yet humble tone is a witness for our Lord.

— Our Manner: Do we carry ourselves in a graceful, lady-like manner? Are we polite and respectful? These things are also a light to the world.

— Our Attitudes: What speaks more than our attitude? We can be a witness through our responses, our servanthood, our heart towards our authorities, and so many other aspects of our spirit. Is your attitude positive, content, joyful, loving, accepting of circumstances, full of faith, and Christ-like? Does your face glow with the spirit of Christ that comes from a right attitude, which comes from a heart submitted to God? Does your countenance radiate Christ?

When we let our light shine, our lives can bless younger girls as well. That is a very rewarding aspect of being a radiant princess of our heavenly King. Sometimes younger girls have told me that they are blessed by observing my life. Whenever

I hear this, I am deeply humbled that the Lord would use me to minister to their lives—especially when I do not "feel like" a blessing—and I realize the responsibility I have to *"be an example of the believers, in word, in conversation, in charity, in spirit, in faith, in purity"* (I Timothy 4:12). This example must be the work of God, not of ourselves, and when someone is blessed by our example, all glory is God's!

Under the blessing of your and her parents, mentor and invest in a younger girl. Share with her what the Lord is teaching you. When she shares questions and struggles she is going through, point her to the Lord and to her authorities, while sharing wisdom from the Word of God and from what the Lord has taught you. If you allow the Lord to minister to others through your life, you will find yourself drawn nearer to Him as you find in Him your source of strength; you will be stretched and challenged; you will be immensely blessed.

Also, remember that younger girls have a tendency to copy those they look up to. Live above reproach, by the grace of God. Evaluate your speech—is it a Christ-like example to be using idle, thoughtless words and phrases? How much we all admire a godly girl with refined speech! Consider your clothing, actions, attitude, and the focus of your life. Are you causing anyone to stumble by your example, or are others being drawn more closely to Christ through your life? Can others see Jesus in you?

Another area in which we can be a light to the world is in using witnessing opportunities. Sharing Jesus with others is another blessing in itself. You will never regret it, though it may be difficult at first to open your mouth to testify for Christ. We do not find it difficult to talk about friends who are important to us, do we? Then why are we ashamed of telling others about the greatest Friend of all, the One Who should be most important to us?

I am blessed to have a weekly witnessing opportunity. Every Tuesday evening, we go out on the streets of our city or door to door. We hand out gospel tracts and talk to people about the Lord. It has been a stretching experience for my faith, and so often I have cried out to the Lord for wisdom in what to say, and how to display Christ through my life. Yet, it has also been very enriching. If you have a regular witnessing opportunity and your parents bless your involvement in it, I encourage you to do share the Gospel! If you do not have such an opportunity, you can still use other opportunities. Leave tracts when you go places in town. Testify about your Lord to people you meet, even in "small" ways. One comment can plant a seed in someone's heart. Reach out to those you see who are hurting, burdened, and purposeless.

When the true Light shines in your heart, you may be surprised how many opportunities come your way to testify to the Lost, minister to the hurting, and bless other believers. You will find life to be enriching as the Lord pours these blessings upon your life. May the Lord bless you as you seek to walk as a radiant light to the world.

KARISSA HIEBERT (19) *is a second-oldest daughter and has three brothers and four sisters. She lives in Manitoba with her family. Her desire is to love her Lord Jesus with all her heart, to serve her family with joy, and to portray the spirit of Christ to all around her.*

"Make the most of what little Christian life you have;
be thankful God has given you so much,
cherish it, pray over it, and guard it like the apple of your eye.
Imperceptibly, but it surely will grow
& keep growing, for this is its nature."[1]

[ELIZABETH PRENTISS]

"We hear the summons of God to love Him with
all our heart and soul and mind and strength.
But do we ever rise to that totality of affection and devotion?
We groan even as we take fresh resolves:
'Not that I have already obtained this or am already perfect,
but I press on to make it my own, because Christ Jesus has made me His own'
(Philippians 3:12). That very statement is the key to endurance & joy."[2]

[JOHN PIPER]

CHAPTER TEN

BOUQUET
of BEAUTY

$\mathcal{I}$ LOVE FLOWERS—picking them, arranging them, and enjoying their vibrant hues. They add a beautiful touch to any yard and a simple little bouquet brightens an entire room.

As much as I enjoy flowers, I dislike the labor that goes into producing such beauty—getting my hands dirty to plant and thin out plants, or worse yet, the sweaty task of weeding. Good gardeners, like my mother, reply to my complaints, "It is worth it!"

The Christian's life is a similar beauty. We see the bounteous fruit of Christ in the lives of more mature believers. We witness the beautiful transformation that God can make in the life of one who has wholly surrendered his heart's throne. We crave this abundant fruit in our own life; we dedicate ourself to Christ, making a burning resolution to live for Him. But as soon as we start out on the heaven-bound journey, we meet relentless trials, pains, vicious temptations, discouraging setbacks, and wearying irritations. We see how vigorously our sinful nature contends for its selfish desires. Wiping the sweat from our brow, we squint ahead into the unrevealing, winding path. The way is indistinguishable and looks wearisome. When will we reach that beautiful Christ-like fruit? Why is it so hard to put down our selfish desires? Everything seems painful and forbidding; the beautiful fruit that we so craved dims...and we begin to wonder, "Is it worth it?"

Every minute, we meet our sinful nature. Every hour, we face trials. Every day, we fail. We learn as did Paul,[3] that when we want to do good, instead, we do wrong. We feel defeated by our failures, yet we must not become discouraged. Looking only to Jesus, we must press forward.[4]

Christ takes all of His children whom He loves through this constant refining process; every Christian battles his own sinful nature while being transformed into Christ's image. *"But He knoweth the way that I take: when He hath tried me, I shall come forth as gold"* (Job 23:10). Has it occurred to you that those Christ-like lives you admire went through the same trials you daily face? Sometimes, it has seemed that Christians I knew were so refined and godly, while I struggled behind, dragging my feet through constant spiritual failures, and recommitments. As I realized that I am not the only one experiencing the breath-taking upward climb toward Christ-like character, my journey seemed much easier.

The Lord has also shown me the relieving fact that He refines me through these trials—and even better, through my *weaknesses* He becomes big in my life! *"My strength is made perfect in weakness. Most gladly therefore will I rather glory in my infirmities, that the power of Christ may rest upon me. Therefore I take pleasure in infirmities, in reproaches, in necessities, in persecutions, in distresses for Christ's sake: for when I am weak, then am I strong"* (II Corinthians 12:9-10). Through my very helplessness, Jesus is glorified; through my failures I learn to rely on His stable presence; through my inability, He is made victor. What a blessed thought!

Sister, I encourage you to focus on and trust the Lord Jesus Christ to do a beautiful work in your life. Surrender yourself to Him, and keep

CHAPTER TEN — *Bouquet of Beauty*

your eyes on Him. It will not be easy—everyday, several times a day, you must repent of your weaknesses and resolve to press forward once again with His help. Do not become discouraged; do not let your eyes wander to the obstacles. Simply trust Him, Who is more than able to do what He promised in Hebrews 13:21, to *"make you perfect in every good work to do his will, working in you that which is wellpleasing in his sight."* It will be so worth the struggle—for in Revelation 22:12, Jesus urges us toward the reward that is awaiting us, *"Behold, I come quickly; and my reward is with me, to give every man according as his work shall be."* According to our labors will our crown be.

Let us press upward together, living each day for the glory of God. This wonderful mission begins right in our home, doing the things He has called us to do. The world around us can be changed because of our humble obedience to our Lord—our simple obedience to become pillars in our family's home. May we each be able to give account someday when we meet our Lord Jesus, "I was a faithful daughter." Blessings to you as you press on *"toward the mark for the prize of the high calling of God in Christ Jesus"* (Philippians 3:14).

on my shelf... RELATED RESOURCES

-- *Stepping Heavenward* by Mrs. Elizabeth Prentiss (Keepers of the Faith, P.O. Box 100, Ironwood, MI 49938; www.keepersofthefaith.com)

-- *Beautiful Girlhood* revised by Karen Andreola (Light of Faith Resources, 1715 S. Porter Avenue, Joplin, MO 64804; 888.78.LIGHT; www.lightoffaith.com)

-- *The Hope Chest: A Legacy of Love* by Mrs. Rebekah Wilson (Hope Chest Legacy, P.O. Box 1398, Littlerock, CA 93543; www.hopechestlegacy.com)

𝒥 HAVE BEEN GREATLY blessed by the examples of godly daughterhood that Lolly and her older sister, Sharia, have been. It has been incredibly encouraging to see the fruit they have reaped because they wisely invested as girls. I have witnessed the faithfulness of God in these dear young ladies' lives as they lived wholeheartedly for Him and honored their parents.

In God's providence, Sharia and Lolly married two brothers. They each have been blessed with many little ones, who they are training in the ways of the Lord. I am excited to share what Lolly, now as a young wife and mother, has shared here. She has much wisdom to impart to us girls—heed and apply her words of experience today during your youth.

—Sarah Lee

a godly homemaker...
LOLLY B. HALE

𝒥 HAVE realized what a responsibility it is to be a godly wife and mother. It takes much more than meets the eye. All those secret times of prayer you slip away for, all those discontented thoughts you refuse to dwell on, all those little offenses you forget and forgive—these are what make a godly wife by God's grace, and the reward reaped will be a godly family. Is that worth it? To a godly woman, it is.

It is relatively easy for me to look back and remember my life at home as a daughter, as it was not long ago. It is amazing what a difference a few years of marriage has made in my life, and how the transition from daughterhood to wife and motherhood can be very fast...for me, it meant three babies before our third anniversary!

I am sure we all can think of different qualities that are essential for godly wifehood and motherhood. I could never list them all, but I would like to share three virtues that are key to starting a happy marriage. These may seem like simple things, but much of life's happiness is contingent upon how simple qualities are fulfilled in our lives.

Personal Relationship with the Lord

Cultivate your relationship with the Lord now. It will not improve on its own by you sitting around dreaming about what a godly wife and mother you will make someday. Let me give you a glimpse into reality...

You will not have the liberty to slip off into the woods in the evening to talk with the Lord, when your husband is home and needs his "keeper at home" to be there for him.

Do you suppose it will be easier to wake up to an alarm for morning devotions when you are married than it is now as a daughter? Have you ever considered how tempting it might be to justify sleeping in as a wife, because your parents are not making you get up? You will not have morning devotion times all by yourself anymore as a wife and mommy. Your husband will be a constant friend that you love sharing your devotional time with, and morning devotions can easily be "chatted away" until it is time to start the day.

When you have little ones vying for your attention, plus house work, dinner preparation, doing that little duty your husband requested before he left—oh yes, and that scrapbooking project is daily getting further behind!—do you think it is natural to pull out your Bible and sit quietly before the Lord because you did not "connect" with Him earlier that morning?

I am thankful my parents made daily devotions a part of our family schedule as I was growing up, so it became a habit in my life, but I must admit that even with this habit strongly impressed into my life for years, I still struggle with making it a priority. Make it a must, girls! There is no way to walk uprightly as a daughter, let alone a wife and mother, unless you are feeding at the King's table.

True Love

True love sounds easy for a girl excitedly anticipating marriage someday, but let's remind ourselves of what true love is. Love is not a feeling; it is a choice. Sometimes love feels loving, and other times it does not. For example, I recall as a girl at home, taking my mother by surprise by grabbing her in a big hug and then jovially excusing myself by saying, "Sorry! I just had a burst of love for you!" Now, that was a moment when I "felt" loving. At another time when my mother would just happen to frustrate me, I might not have had quite the same burst of love for her, though I loved my mother just as dearly. Though our love does not change, our feelings do.

Likewise, there are countless times in a marriage when as a wife I have feelings of love for my husband that are very special, and there are other times when I do not feel quite so lovely. Here are some examples.

— What about when you see another girl that is prettier than you, and you are worried your husband will compare her to you? Love envieth not.

— When your husband is having a hard afternoon, will you reach beyond yourself and your own difficult afternoon to be there for him? Love suffers long and is kind.

— Do you mop the floor, do the paperwork, or wash the car so your husband will notice—or out of love for him, whether he notices or not? Love vaunteth not itself, is not puffed up.

— How will you respond when your husband does not come home to dinner on time and the lovely meal that you made "just for him" (or was it for your own self-esteem) is not fresh and hot anymore? Love is not easily provoked.

— What about when your husband makes a bad decision? Do you still rejoice in the truth of the wonderful man God has given you? Love rejoiceth not in iniquity, but rejoiceth in the truth.

Be honest with yourself. "Behold, thou desirest truth in the inward parts" (Psalm 51:6). Who you really are will come out in your marriage. I have been realizing more and more that my marriage is for my perfection, so I can be conformed more and more to the image of Christ. If the Lord truly loves me, He will stop at nothing to perform His good work in me— even by testing me in all my weakest areas so I can become that "perfect wife" of which I always dreamed.

Contentment

"Godliness with contentment is great gain" (I Timothy 6:6). The Lord blessed me before my marriage with enjoying my role at home as a blessed daughter and big sister. I loved being at home. I enjoyed life. I spent time helping my mother be a keeper at home, investing in my siblings, and serving others outside our home. I did not waste a lot of time reading and dreaming about my future. I was content. Oh, how I value that attitude with which God blessed me! It has helped me so much in my married life. There was a common phrase in our home amongst us girls and our mother, and now I am convinced of the truth of it. "If you're not content at home, you will not be content when you're married."

The Lord has blessed me so much; there are no words to express His goodness to me, yet, every day I must choose to be content in His goodness. If I begin complaining in my heart about my present state, it certainly becomes very distasteful. But, to the contrary, when I am rejoicing where the Lord has me, everything becomes bright and beautiful. It is all your point of view, girls, and you can choose to have a happy viewpoint if you want to. Everyone who comes in contact with you will appreciate it, especially your family who lives with you!

I love being married. God gave me a very special husband and a very special life, but that's my point of view. Like the plaque in my parent's house says, "Attitude is everything–choose a good one."

MRS. LOLLY HALE (25) lives with her little family in Palmer, Alaska. Lolly is the second-eldest of nine homeschooled children. After graduating from high school in 2002, she stayed at home to assist her mother with domestic duties, help homeschool her siblings, and wait on the Lord's timing for His plans for her future. In 2004, Joseph and Lolly met, and they were married in 2006. The Lord has blessed them with three sons: Benaiah, Caleb, and Titus.

ENDNOTES

PREFACE — As Cornerstones
[1] I Corinthians 7:36-38
[2] By the term "world," we are referring to the culture that is not in submission with God. "Love not the world, neither the things that are in the world. If any man love the world, the love of the Father is not in him. For all that is in the world, the lust of the flesh, and the lust of the eyes, and the pride of life, is not of the Father, but is of the world. And the world passeth away, and the lust thereof: but he that doeth the will of God abideth forever." (1 John 2:15-17)
[4] Noah Webster's *American Dictionary of the English Language*, 1828
[5] Ibid.
[6] Proverbs 14:1

CHAPTER ONE — An Abundant Season
[1] Biblically, a woman is not to go out of the God-given protection of her father, but it is not implied that a woman cannot go outside of the home. She can efficiently work for her father and represent him wherever she goes with his approval. Her main sphere of influence is in the home, where the majority of her time is spent.

CHAPTER TWO — In My Father's House
[1] "Victory for Daughters" audio, by Kelly Brown and Sarah, Rebekah, & Hannah Zes (Vision Forum Inc.: San Antonio, TX)
[2] If you do not have a father, God places you under the authority of your mother and older brothers (Genesis 24 and 29)
[3] Also Ephesians 5:22-4 and 1 Peter 3:1,3-6
[4] Proverbs 31:11
[5] "Understanding the Biblical Vision for Fathers & Daughters" audio, Doug Phillips (Vision Forum Inc.: San Antonio, TX)
[6] "Victory for Daughters" audio, by Brown & Zes (Vision Forum Inc.: San Antonio, TX)
[7] McCullough, David, *Mornings on Horseback* (Simon Schuster, 1981)

CHAPTER THREE — Our Parents' Joy
[1] Exodus 20:12
[2] Also Proverbs 3:1,4
[3] Proverbs 3:21-24, 2:1,5
[4] Those who have godly parents should never take this blessing for granted!
[5] 1 Corinthians 13:3-8
[6] Noah Webster's *American Dictionary of the English Language*, 1828
[7] Proverbs 23:25
[8] Bahnsen, Greg, *By This Standard*, pp. 29 (Institute for Christian Economics: Tyler, TX, 1985)
[9] I considered any girl who was a few years older than I to be an "older girl," and I greatly respected them. When they did not dress modestly or act properly, I was disappointed in their example, because I expected them to be mature.

CHAPTER FOUR — The Family Sister
[1] Botkin, Anna Sofia & Elizabeth, *So Much More*, pp. 204 (Vision Forum Inc.: San Antonio, TX, 2005)
[2] Dr. S. M. Davis, SolveFamilyProblems.com
[3] Mally, *Making Brothers and Sisters Best Friends*, pp. 208 (Tomorrow's Forefathers: Cedar Rapids, IA, 2002)

CHAPTER FIVE — Pillars of Strength
[1] Meyers, Deana, *I Will Give You The Rain*, pp. 34 (Quiet Harvest: Kansas City, KS, 2009)
[2] John 15:4 and Philippians 1:6
[3] John 15:8
[4] Psalm 63:6
[5] Hiebert, Karissa, "Quiet Time" (*The King's Blooming Rose* Magazine: Volume 4 Issue 1)

[6] Prentiss, Elizabeth, *Stepping Heavenward* (Keepers of the Faith: Ironwood, MI)
[7] Many sources offer Bible recordings in MP3 format, which have been helpful to me in memorizing Scripture.
[8] Performed by the Serven family in four-part harmony; these helped my family learn to harmonize (*www.genevanfoundation.com*).
[9] *KBR Ministries* offers a Scripture Memory calendar which schedules the memorization of Bible books (check availability at *www.kingsbloomingrose.com*).
[10] Prentiss, Elizabeth, *Stepping Heavenward* (Keepers of the Faith: Ironwood, MI)
[11] One example is found in Exodus 15
[12] Henry, Matthew, *Matthew Henry's Commentary on the Whole Bible*
[13] Ephesians 6:11
[14] Lindsey, Mrs. Connie, "Quiet Guidance" (*The King's Blooming Rose* Magazine: Volume 4 Issue 1)

CHAPTER SIX
— A Humble Maidservant

[1] Prentiss, Elizabeth, *Stepping Heavenward* (Keepers of the Faith: Ironwood, MI)
[2] Thomas, W., *The Saving Life of Christ*, pp. 19 (Zondervan: Grand Rapids, MI, 1961)
[3] Ibid.
[4] Osebreh, Jessica, "Humility" (*The King's Blooming Rose* Magazine: Volume 4 Issue 3)
[5] Havergal, Francis, *Kept for the Master's Use*, pp. 54 (Keepers of the Faith: Ironwood, MI; 2000 reprint of 1879 edition)
[6] Psalm 104:33

CHAPTER SEVEN
— The Spotless Maiden

[1] Kempis, Thomas, *The Imitation of Christ* (Moody Publishing: Chicago, IL)
[2] I Peter 3:4
[3] Doug Phillips, *www.visionforum.org*
[4] Genesis 3:16
[5] Cassidy, Molly, "Emotional Freedom: Being Ardent Lovers of Jesus Christ" (*HopeChest* Magazine: Volume 13 Number 1)
[6] As translated in II Corinthians 11:2, Titus 2:5, and I Peter 3:2
[7] Mally, Sarah, *Before You Meet Prince Charming*, pp. 91 (Tomorrow's Forefathers: Cedar Rapids, IA, 2006; *www.radiantpurity.com*)
[8] Von Schmid, Christoph, *Basket of Flowers* (reprinted by Lamplighter Publishing: Waverly, PA)

CHAPTER EIGHT
— The Appointed Time

[1] Havergal, Francis, *Kept for the Master's Use*, pp. 25 (Keepers of the Faith: Ironwood, MI, 2000 reprint of 1879 edition)
[2] Romans 3:12
[3] Psalm 26:2

CHAPTER NINE
— Reflecting The Light

[1] Hosea 7:13
[2] See also Romans 3:19, Revelation 20:15
[3] Havergal, Francis, *Kept for the Master's Use*, pp. 111 (Keepers of the Faith: Ironwood, MI, 2000 reprint of 1879 edition)
[4] As a note, if all of our friends are peers and these relationships are not focused on Christ, we will not be challenged spiritually. Proverbs 27:17 says, "*Iron sharpeneth iron; so a man sharpeneth the countenance of his friend.*" Often we will find this wisdom from those who are older than ourselves; Titus 2:3-4 instructs, "*The aged women likewise, that they be in behavior as becometh holiness... that they may teach the young women...*" We should seek out these Christian women and learn from their lives.

CHAPTER TEN — Bouquet of Beauty

[1] Prentiss, Elizabeth, *Stepping Heavenward* (Keepers of the Faith: Ironwood, MI)
[2] Piper, John, *The Passion of Christ*, pp. 48 (Crossway Books: Wheaton, IL, 2004)
[3] Romans 7:15
[4] Galatians 6:9

Note: Use discretion regarding the recommended resources; we do not claim to endorse everything in other sources. Some may be targeted towards older readers. Please let your parents advise you on what material is profitable for you.

the story behind THIS BOOK

*M*Y DAD HAS ALWAYS encouraged me to write a book, but the task of filling an entire book was overwhelming to me. The Lord had other plans though! In August of 2008, I came across a book written by a sixteen-year-old girl. I thought, *That's amazing...but it's too late for me to write one while I am sixteen, since I'm almost seventeen!* Around the same time, I bought a booklet written for young ladies. The next week, God gave me the idea to write a small booklet to encourage girls to serve and enjoy their families. As I collected my thoughts, the "small book" grew bigger than I expected and turned into quite a large project.

In 2007, the Lord gave me great joy in being a daughter in my family. A phrase that kept running through my mind was "the family daughter"—not to just accept being the oldest daughter, but to embrace this responsibility. He also gave me a desire to encourage other girls to do the same. When God led me to write a book, I was amazed to see He had already given me the title and message.

I am so thankful for the countless hours my parents have spent editing this manuscript, and the input they have shared with me on the topics addressed. May God be praised!   —Sarah Lee

credits PHOTOGRAPHY

©SarahLee Photography unless otherwise noted

FRONT COVER · by Nathan T. Bryant
AUTHOR'S PHOTO · by Thomas E. Bryant
INTERIOR · PAGE 15: Sarah, & Rachael B.; PAGE 21: Dana, Jonathan & Nathan B.; PAGE 29: Laura Boggs, ©Sara Boggs; PAGE 51: Samuel B. & Joshua Bodenheimer; PAGE 52: Tom, Sarah, and Dana B.; PAGE 69: Brytni and Bellhannah Cutler; PAGE 78: Rachael and Sarah B.; PAGE 80: Bryant Siblings; PAGE 93: Rachael B.; PAGE 117: Sarah B.; PAGE 128: Sarah B. with harp; PAGE 135: Bryants and Wahlquists fellowship; PAGE 157: Sarah Serven, Rebecca (Serven) Loomis, Sarah B., Lydia & Susanna Hayden, Beth (Serven) Ten Dolle; PAGE 171: Tom and Jonathan B. fishing; PAGE 190: Samuel B.; PAGE 191: A Rose; PAGE 194: Lolly & Joseph Hale and Joshua & Sharia Hale, ©Buckingham Family.

about the AUTHOR

SARAH L. BRYANT is the daughter of Tom & Dana Bryant and has five siblings: Brandon (25), Nathan (14), Jonathan (12), Rachael (10) and Samuel (8). Sarah enjoys working with her family, studying theology and Constitutional Law, digital photography, graphic design, playing piano and harp, sewing, and publishing *The King's Blooming Rose* magazine. At the time she began writing this book, Sarah was 16. Since graduation in 2009, she has invested time in home repair, learning various new skills, working in the family business, and correspondence college courses. She desires to be a wife and mother someday, if the Lord wills.

The Bryant family homeschools on an acreage in Kansas, where they operate a family farm, producing various meat and dairy products. They desire to raise a generation for the glory of God.

WWW.BRYANTFAMILYFARM.COM

• ENCOURAGING GIRLS TO GROW IN THEIR WALK WITH CHRIST! •

"That I may publish with the voice of thanksgiving." (Psalm 26:7)

The King's Blooming Rose Magazine

Would you like to receive encouragement regularly in your Christian walk? Would you like to meet other Christian young ladies and families serving our King? We invite you to join us on our journey to biblical womanhood!

The King's Blooming Rose is a quarterly magazine published for the encouragement of girls in their Christian walk. Each issue features a daughterhood-related theme and includes inspiring articles, homemaking tips and much more. We look forward to hearing from you, and while you are writing, include a brief introduction of yourself!

The Young Maid: Compiled from KBR Magazine

Would you like to redeem the time as a young lady and learn skills that would benefit you as a future wife and mother? 'The Young Maid' is a question-and-answer column featuring homemaking-related topics in *KBR Magazine*. Find two years of this column compiled into one volume—this 20-page booklet.

KBR Forum: Monthly Thoughts

We post a monthly article for the encouragement of daughters in their walk with the Lord on our website. Readers are welcome to share encouragement and a personal testimony.

Check our website for more encouraging resources and articles!

WWW.KINGSBLOOMINGROSE.COM

ORDER FORM

Feel free to copy this order form. Make checks or money orders payable to Sarah Bryant; mail to 21350 Springdale Road, Easton KS 66020 or order online at *www.KingsBloomingRose.com*.

The Family Daughter: Becoming Pillars of Strength in Our Father's House
_____$12.00 each   SUBTOTAL:_____

The Young Maid: Compiled from KBR *Magazine*
_____$4.00 each   SUBTOTAL:_____

The King's Blooming Rose Quarterly Magazine
_____$7.00 for One-Year USA Subscription
_____$10.00 for One-Year Canadian Subscription
_____$12.00 for One-Year Foreign Country Subscription
                                                   SUBTOTAL:_____

USA SHIPPING RATES
$0.01-15.00..........add $3.00
$15.01-30.00..........add $5.00
$30.01-50.00..........add $7.00
over $50.01................free

Please double rates for foreign orders.

When figuring your shipping price, do not include the price of magazine items; shipping has already been included in subscription rates.

BOOK TOTAL:_____
+SHIPPING:_____
=GRAND TOTAL:_____

SHIP TO

Name:_____Age:_____
Address:_____
City:_____State:_____Zip:_____
Phone:_____
Email:_____
Where did you buy this book?_____
Comments:_____
_____
_____
_____